LIFE APPLICATION BIBLE

Gospel of mark

TYNDALE HOUSE PUBLISHERS, INC.
WHEATON, ILLINOIS

First printing, July 1986

Gospel of Mark, from
Life Application Bible

The text of the *Life Application Bible* is from
The Living Bible, copyright © 1971 by Tyndale
House Publishers, Wheaton, Illinois 60189. All rights reserved.
The Living Bible is a compilation of the Scripture
portions previously published by Tyndale House Publishers
under the following titles: *Living Letters,* 1962;
Living Prophecies, 1965; *Living Gospels,* 1966;
Living Psalms and Proverbs, 1967; *Living Lessons of
Life and Love,* 1968; *Living Books of Moses,* 1969;
Living History of Israel, 1970.

Life Application Notes and Bible Helps copyright ©
1986 by Youth for Christ/USA. Maps copyright © 1986
by Tyndale House Publishers, Inc. All rights reserved.

ISBN 0-8423-2565-4
Library of Congress Catalog Card Number 86-50730

Printed in the United States of America

Have you ever opened your Bible and asked the following:

- What does this passage really mean?
- How does it apply to my life?
- Why does some of the Bible seem irrelevant?
- What do these ancient cultures have to do with today?
- I love God; why can't I understand what he is saying to me through his Word?
- What's going on in the lives of these Bible people?.

Many Christians do not read the Bible regularly. Why? Because in the pressures of daily living they cannot find a connection between the timeless principles of Scripture and the ever-present problems of day-by-day living.

It is ironic that so many Christians have a Bible, but so few of them know how to use it to change their lives. This is why the *Life Application Bible* was developed. God urges us to *apply* his Word (Isaiah 42:23; 1 Corinthians 10:11; 2 Thessalonians 3:4), but too often we stop at accumulating Bible knowledge. The *Life Application Bible* shows how to put into practice what we have learned.

Applying God's Word is a vital part of one's relationship with God; it is the evidence that we are obeying him. The difficulty in applying the Bible is not with the Bible itself, but with the reader's inability to bridge the gap between the past and present, the conceptual and practical. When we don't or can't do this, spiritual dryness, shallowness, and indifference are the results. A gulf opens up between faith and practice. Although we may be familiar with a passage of Scripture, we don't apply it in daily life.

The words of Scripture itself cry out to us, "Won't even one of you apply these lessons" (Isaiah 42:23)? The *Life Application Bible* does just that. Developed by an interdenominational team of pastors, scholars, family counselors, and a national organization dedicated to promoting God's Word and spreading the Gospel, the *Life Application Bible* took many years to complete, and all the work was reviewed by a renowned theologian, Dr. Kenneth Kantzer.

The *Life Application Bible* does what a good study Bible should—it helps you understand the context of a passage, gives important background and historical information, explains difficult words and phrases, and helps you see the interrelationship of Scripture. But it does much more. The *Life Application Bible* goes deeper into God's Word, helping you discover the timeless truth being communicated, see the relevance for your life, and make a personal application. While other study Bibles attempt application, over 75% of this Bible is application-oriented. The study notes answer the questions, "So what?" and "What does this passage mean to me, my family, my friends, my job, my neighborhood, my church, my country?"

Imagine reading a familiar passage of Scripture and gaining fresh insight, as if it were the first time you had ever read it. How much richer your life would be if you left each Bible reading with a new perspective

and a small change for the better? A small change every day adds up to a changed life—and that is the very purpose of Scripture.

When you read the *Life Application Bible* your goal shouldn't be just to learn more. The notes are not the last word; rather, they should spark the beginning of a lifetime adventure of growing with God and deepening your spiritual character.

The best way to define application is to first determine what it is *not*. Application is *not* just accumulating knowledge. This helps us discover and understand facts and concepts, but it stops there. History is filled with philosophers who knew what the Bible said, but failed to apply it to their lives, keeping them from believing and changing. Many think that understanding is the end goal of Bible study, but it is really only the beginning.

Application is *not* just illustration. Illustration only tells us how someone else handled a similar situation. While we may empathize with that person, we still have little direction for our personal situation.

Application is *not* just making a passage "relevant." Making the Bible relevant only helps us to see that the same lessons that were true in Bible times are true today; it does not show us how to apply them to the problems and pressures of our individual lives.

What, then, is application? Application begins by knowing and understanding God's Word and its timeless truths. *But you cannot stop there.* If you do, God's Word may not change your life, and it may become dull, difficult, tedious, and tiring. A good application focuses the truth of God's Word, shows the reader what to do about what is being read, and motivates the reader to respond to what God is teaching. All three are essential to application.

Application is putting into practice what we already know (see Mark 4:24 and Hebrews 5:14) and answering the question, "So what?" by confronting us with the right questions and motivating us to take action (see 1 Timothy 4:8 and James 4:20). Application is deeply personal— unique for each individual. It is making a relevant truth a personal truth, and involves developing a strategy and action plan to live your life in harmony with the Bible. It is the biblical "how to" of life.

You may ask, "How can your application notes be relevant to *my* life?" Each application note has three parts: (1) an *explanation* that ties the note directly to the Scripture passage and sets up the truth that is being taught, (2) the *bridge* which explains the timeless truth and makes it relevant for today, (3) the *application* which shows you how to take the timeless truth and apply it to your personal situation. No note, by itself, can apply Scripture directly to your life. It can only teach, direct, lead, guide, inspire, recommend, and urge. It can give you the resources and direction you need to apply the Bible; but only you can take these resources and put them into practice.

A good note, therefore, should not only give you knowledge and understanding, but point you to application. Before you buy a study Bible, you should evaluate the notes and ask the following questions: (1) Does the note contain enough information to help me understand the point of the Scripture passage? (2) Does the note assume I know too much? (3) Does the note avoid denominational bias? (4) Do the notes touch most of life's experiences? (5) Does the note help me *apply* God's Word?

STUDY NOTES

In addition to providing the reader with many application notes, the *Life Application Bible* offers several explanatory notes, which are notes that help the reader understand culture, history, context, difficult-to-understand passages, background, places, theological concepts, and the relationship of various passages in Scripture to other passages. Maps, charts, and diagrams are also found in the footnotes, on the same page as the passages to which they relate. For an example of an application note, see Mark 15:47. For an example of an explanatory note, see Mark 11:1, 2.

BOOK INTRODUCTIONS

The Book Introductions are divided into several easy-to-find parts; many are found in no other study Bible.

Timeline. This puts the Bible book into its historical setting. It lists the key events of each book and the date when they occurred.

Vital Statistics. This is a list of straight facts about the book—those pieces of information you need to know at a glance.

Overview. This is a summary of the book with general lessons and applications that can be learned from the book as a whole.

Blueprint. This is the outline of the book. It is printed in easy-to-understand language and is designed for easy memorization. To the right of each main heading is a key lesson that is taught in that particular section.

Megathemes. This section gives the main themes of the Bible book, explains their significance, and then tells why they are still important for us today.

Maps. This shows the key places found in that book and retells the story of the book from a geographical point of view.

OUTLINE

The *Life Application Bible* has a new, custom-made outline that was designed specifically from an application point of view. Several unique features should be noted:

1. To avoid confusion and to aid memory work, each book outline has only three levels for headings. Main outline heads are marked with a capital letter. Sub-heads are marked by a number. Minor, explanatory heads have no letter or number.
2. Each main outline head marked by a letter also has a brief paragraph

below it summarizing the Bible text and offering a general
application.
3. Parallel passages are listed where they apply in the Gospels and in
the books of Samuel, Kings, and Chronicles.

HARMONY OF THE GOSPELS

A harmony of the Gospels was developed specifically for this Bible. It is
the first harmony that has ever been incorporated into the Bible text.
Through a unique and simple numbering system, you can read any
Gospel account and see just where you are in relation to the entire life of
Christ. The harmony is located in the back of this book and explained in
detail there.

PROFILE NOTES

Another unique feature of this Bible is the profiles of over 150 Bible
people, including their strengths and weaknesses, greatest
accomplishments and mistakes, and key lessons from their lives. The
profiles of these people are found in the Bible books where their stories
occur.

MAPS

The *Life Application Bible* has more maps than any other Bible. A
thorough and comprehensive Bible atlas is built right into each Bible
book. There are three kinds of maps: (1) A book introduction map,
telling the story of that Bible book. (2) Thumbnail maps in the notes,
plotting most geographic movements in the Bible. (3) Full-color
reference maps in the back of the Bible, showing larger relationships.

CHARTS AND DIAGRAMS

Dozens of charts and diagrams are included to help the reader better
visualize difficult concepts or relationships. Most charts not only present
the needed information, but show the significance of the information as
well.

CROSS REFERENCES

An updated, exhaustive cross reference system in the margins of the
Bible text helps the reader find related passages quickly.

INDEX TO NOTES

This Gospel of Mark contains a complete index to all the notes. With its
emphasis on application, it is helpful for Bible study, sermon
preparation, teaching, or personal study.

Gospel of mark

MARK

VITAL STATISTICS

PURPOSE:
To present the person, work, and teachings of Jesus.

AUTHOR:
John Mark. He was not one of the twelve disciples but he accompanied Paul on his first missionary journey (Acts 13:13).

TO WHOM WRITTEN:
The Christians in Rome, where he wrote the Gospel

DATE WRITTEN:
Between A.D. 55 and 65

SETTING:
The Roman Empire under Tiberius Caesar. The Empire, with its common language and excellent transportation and communication systems, was ripe to hear Jesus' message, which spread quickly from nation to nation.

KEY VERSE:
"For even I, the Messiah, am not here to be served, but to help others, and to give my life as a ransom for many" (10:45).

KEY PEOPLE:
Jesus, the twelve disciples, Pilate, the Jewish religious leaders

KEY PLACES:
Capernaum, Nazareth, Caesarea Philippi, Jericho, Bethany, Mount of Olives, Jerusalem, Golgotha

SPECIAL FEATURES:
Mark was the first Gospel written. The other Gospels quote all but 31 verses of Mark. Mark records more miracles than does any other Gospel.

EVERYONE wants to be a winner. Losers are those who finish any less than first. In direct contrast are the words of Jesus, "And whoever wants to be greatest of all must be the slave of all. For even I, the Messiah, am not here to be served, but to help others, and to give my life as a ransom for many" (10:44, 45). Jesus *is* the greatest—God incarnate, our Messiah—but he entered history as a servant.

This is the message of Mark. Written to encourage Roman Christians and to prove beyond a doubt that Jesus is the Messiah, Mark presents a rapid succession of vivid pictures of Jesus in action—his true identity revealed by what he does, not by what he says (18 miracles are described, and only four parables). It is Jesus on the move. As you read Mark, be ready for action, be open for God's move into your life, and be challenged to move into your world to serve.

Omitting the birth of Jesus, Mark begins with John the Baptist's preaching. Then, moving quickly past Jesus' baptism, temptation in the desert, and call of the disciples, Mark takes us directly into his public ministry. We see Jesus confronting a demon, healing a leper, and forgiving and healing the paralyzed man lowered into his presence by friends.

Next, Jesus called Matthew and had dinner with him and his questionable associates. This incident initiated the conflict with the Pharisees and other religious leaders who condemned him for eating with sinners and breaking the Sabbath.

In chapter 4, Mark pauses to give a sample of Jesus' teaching—the parable of the sower and the illustration of the mustard seed—and then plunges back into the action. Jesus calmed the waves, cast out demons, and healed Jairus' daughter.

After returning to Nazareth for a few days and experiencing rejection in his home town, Jesus commissioned the disciples to spread the Good News everywhere. Opposition from Herod and the Pharisees increased and John the Baptist was beheaded, but Jesus continued to move, feeding 5,000, reaching out to the Syrophoenician woman, healing the deaf man, and feeding 4,000.

Finally it was time to confront the disciples with his true identity. Did they really know who he was? Peter proclaimed him Messiah, but then promptly showed he did not understand Jesus' mission. After the transfiguration, Jesus continued to teach and heal, confronting the Pharisees about divorce and the rich young ruler about eternal life. Blind Bartimaeus was healed.

Events rapidly move toward a climax. The Last Supper, the betrayal, the crucifixion, and the resurrection are dramatically portrayed, along with more examples of Jesus' teachings. Mark shows us Jesus—moving, serving, sacrificing, and saving!

THE BLUEPRINT

A. BIRTH AND PREPARATION OF JESUS, THE SERVANT (1:1-13)

Jesus did not arrive unannounced or unexpected. The Old Testament prophets had clearly predicted the coming of a great One, sent by God himself, who would offer salvation and eternal peace to Israel and the entire world. Then came John the Baptist, who announced that the long-awaited Messiah had finally come, and would soon be among the people. In God's work in the world today, Jesus does not come unannounced, or unexpected. Yet many still reject him. We have the witness of the Bible to show the way, but some choose to ignore it as they ignored John the Baptist in his day.

B. MESSAGE AND MINISTRY OF JESUS, THE SERVANT (1:14—13:37)
1. Jesus' ministry in Galilee
2. Jesus' ministry beyond Galilee
3. Jesus' ministry in Jerusalem

Jesus had all the power of almighty God—he raised the dead, gave sight to the blind, restored deformed bodies, and quieted stormy seas. But with all this power, Jesus came to mankind as a servant. We can use his life as a pattern for how to live today. As Jesus served God and others, so should we.

C. DEATH AND RESURRECTION OF JESUS, THE SERVANT (14:1—16:20)

Jesus came as a servant, so many did not recognize or acknowledge him as the Messiah. We, too, must be careful we don't reject God or his will because it doesn't quite fit our image of how God should be.

MEGATHEMES

THEME	EXPLANATION	IMPORTANCE
Jesus Christ	Jesus Christ alone is the Son of God. In Mark, Jesus demonstrates his divinity by overcoming disease, demons, and death. Although he had the power to be king of the earth, Jesus chose to obey the Father and die for us.	When Jesus rose from the dead, he proved that he was God, that he could forgive sin, and that he has the power to change our lives. By trusting in him for forgiveness, we can begin a new life with him as our guide.
Servant	As the "Messiah," Jesus fulfilled the prophecies of the Old Testament by coming to earth. He did not come as a conquering king; he came as a servant. He helped mankind by telling them about God and healing them. Even more, by giving his life as a sacrifice for sin, he did the ultimate act of service.	Because of Jesus' example, we should be willing to serve God and others. Real greatness in Christ's kingdom is shown by service and sacrifice. Ambition, love of power or position, should not be our motive; instead, we should do God's work because we love him.
Pharisees	Although Jesus was popular with the crowds, the religious leaders opposed him. They said they loved God, but they loved power, position, and respectability more than God. As he exposed this hypocrisy, their hatred and jealousy drove them to put Jesus to death.	Jesus' message required a choice: the Pharisees chose to reject him and his message. We face the same choice to accept Jesus or reject him. We must decide how we will respond to his message. Pride in our religious backgrounds must never hinder us from seeing Christ for who he really is.

| *Miracles* | Mark records more of Jesus' miracles than sermons. Jesus is clearly a man of power and action, not just words. Jesus did miracles to convince the people who he was and to teach the disciples his true identity as God. | The more convinced we become that Jesus is God, the more we will see his power and his love. His mighty works show us he is able to save anyone regardless of their past. His miracles of forgiveness bring healing, wholeness, and changed lives to those who trust him. |
| *Spreading the Gospel* | Jesus directed his public ministry to the Jews first. When the Jewish leaders opposed him, Jesus also went to the non-Jewish world, healing and preaching. Roman soldiers, Syrians, and other Gentiles heard the Good News. Many believed and followed him. Jesus' final message to his disciples challenged them to go into all the world and preach the gospel of salvation. | Jesus crossed national, racial, and economic barriers to spread his Good News. Jesus' message of faith and forgiveness is for the whole world not just our church, neighborhood, or nation. We must reach out beyond our own people and needs to fulfill the worldwide vision of Jesus Christ that people everywhere might hear this great message and be saved from sin and death. |

A. BIRTH AND PREPARATION OF JESUS, THE SERVANT (1:1–13)

Mark, the shortest of the four Gospels, opens with Jesus' baptism and temptation. Moving right into action, Mark quickly prepares us for Christ's ministry. The Gospel of Mark is concise, straightforward, and chronological.

John the Baptist prepares the way for Jesus
(16/Matthew 3:1–12; Luke 3:1–18)

1 Here begins the wonderful story of Jesus the Messiah, the Son of God. ² In the book written by the prophet Isaiah, God announced that he would send his Son to earth, and that a special messenger would arrive first to prepare the world for his coming.

³ "This messenger will live out in the barren wilderness," Isaiah said, "and will proclaim that everyone must straighten out his life to be ready for the Lord's arrival."

⁴ This messenger was John the Baptist. He lived in the wilderness and taught that all should be baptized as a public announcement of their decision

1:1
Ps 2:7
Mt 3:1–6, 11
Lk 1:35
3:1–6, 16
Jn 1:34
Rom 8:3
1 Jn 4:15
1:2, 3
Isa 40:3
Mal 3:1
Jn 1:23
1:4
Acts 19:4

1:2 *his Son,* implied.   **1:4** *so that God could forgive them,* literally, "preaching a baptism of repentance for the forgiveness of sins."

1:1 When you experience the excitement of a big event, you naturally want to tell someone. Telling the story can bring back that original thrill as you relive the experience. Reading Mark's first words, you can sense his excitement. Picture yourself in the crowd as Jesus heals and teaches. Imagine yourself as one of the disciples. Respond to his words of love and encouragement. And remember that Jesus came for every man and woman, for us who live today as well as those who lived two thousand years ago.

1:1 Mark was not one of the twelve disciples of Jesus, but he probably knew Jesus personally. He wrote his Gospel in the form of a fast-paced story, like a popular novel. The book portrays Jesus as a man who backed up his words with action that constantly proved who he is— the Son of God. Because he wrote the Gospel for Christians in Rome where many gods were worshiped, Mark wanted them to know that Jesus is *the one true* Son of God.

1:2 Why did Jesus come at this time in history? The entire civilized world was relatively peaceful under Roman rule, travel was easy, and there was a common language. The news about Jesus' life, death, and resurrection could

spread quickly throughout the vast Roman Empire.

In Israel, common men and women were ready for Jesus too. There had been no God-sent prophets for 400 years, since the days of Malachi (who wrote the last book of the Old Testament). There was growing anticipation that a great prophet, or the Messiah mentioned in the Old Testament Scriptures, would soon come (see Luke 3:15).

1:2, 3 Isaiah was one of the greatest prophets of the Old Testament. The second half of the book of Isaiah is devoted to the promise of salvation. Isaiah wrote about the coming of the Messiah, Jesus Christ, and the man who would announce his coming, John the Baptist. John's call for people to "straighten out" their lives meant that they should give up their selfish way of living, renounce sins, seek God's forgiveness, and establish a relationship with almighty God by believing and obeying his words as found in the Bible (Isaiah 1:18–20; 57:15).

1:2, 3 Mark 1:2, 3 is a composite quotation, taken first from Malachi 3:1 and then from Isaiah 40:3. Isaiah is cited first because it was customary for biblical writers to credit the more prominent prophet. The earliest manuscripts read "Isaiah"; later manuscripts read "the prophets."

Modern names and boundaries are shown in gray.

Of the four Gospels, Mark's narrative is the most chronological—that is, most of the stories are positioned in the order they actually occurred. Though the shortest of the four, the Gospel of Mark contains the most events; it is action-packed. Most of this action centers in Galilee, where Jesus began his ministry. Capernaum served as his base of operation (1:21; 2:1; 9:33), from which he would go out to cities like Bethsaida-Julias—where he healed a blind man (8:22ff); Gennesaret— where he performed many healings (6:53ff); Tyre and Sidon (to the far north)—where he cured many, cast out demons, and met the Syrophoenician woman (3:8; 7:24ff); and Caesarea-Philippi—where Peter declared him to be the Messiah (8:27ff). After his ministry in Galilee and the surrounding regions, Jesus headed south for Jerusalem (10:1). Before going there, Jesus told his disciples three times that he would be crucified there and then come back to life. (8:31; 9:31; 10:33, 34).

1:2, 3 Hundreds of years earlier, the prophet Isaiah had predicted that John the Baptist and Jesus would come. How did he know? God promised Isaiah that a Deliverer would come to Israel, and that a voice crying in the wilderness would prepare the way for him. Isaiah's words comforted many people as they looked forward to the Messiah, and knowing that God keeps his promises should comfort us too. Mark wrote much concerning the future, and God will keep these promises. As you read the book, part of God's Word, realize it is more than just a story; God is revealing to you his plans for human history.

1:4 Why does the Gospel of Mark begin with the story of John the Baptist, while not mentioning the story of Jesus' birth? Important Roman officials of this day were always preceded by an announcer or herald. When the herald arrived in town, the people knew that someone of prominence would soon arrive. Since Mark's audience was primarily Roman Christians, he began his book with John the Baptist, the one whose mission it was to announce the coming of Jesus, the most important man who ever lived. Roman Christians wouldn't have been as interested in Jesus' birth as they would be in this herald.

1:4 John chose to live in the wilderness: (1) to get away from distractions so he could hear God's instructions; (2) to capture the undivided attention of the people; (3) to symbolize a sharp break with the hypocrisy of the religious leaders who preferred their luxurious homes and positions of authority over doing God's work; (4) to fulfill Old Testament prophecies which said that John would be a voice "crying in the wilderness" (Isaiah 40:3).

1:4 In John's ministry, baptism was a visible sign that a person had decided to change his or her life, giving up a sinful and selfish way of living and turning to God. John took a known custom and gave it new meaning. The Jews often baptized non-Jews who had converted to Judaism. But to baptize a Jew as a sign of repentance was a radical departure from Jewish custom. The early church took baptism a step further, associating it with Jesus' death and resurrection (see, for example, 1 Peter 3:21).

to turn their backs on sin, so that God could forgive them. ⁵People from Jerusalem and from all over Judea traveled out into the Judean wastelands to see and hear John, and when they confessed their sins he baptized them in the Jordan River. ⁶His clothes were woven from camel's hair and he wore a leather belt; locusts and wild honey were his food. ⁷Here is a sample of his preaching:

"Someone is coming soon who is far greater than I am, so much greater that I am not even worthy to be his slave. ⁸I baptize you with water but he will baptize you with God's Holy Spirit!"

1:6
Lev 11:22
1:7
Jn 1:15
Acts 13:25

1:8
Isa 44:3
Joel 2:28
Acts 2:4; 10:45
11:15, 16
1 Cor 12:13

John baptizes Jesus
(17/Matthew 3:13–17; Luke 3:21, 22)

⁹Then one day Jesus came from Nazareth in Galilee, and was baptized by John there in the Jordan River. ¹⁰The moment Jesus came up out of the water, he saw the heavens open and the Holy Spirit in the form of a dove descending on him, ¹¹ and a voice from heaven said, "You are my beloved Son; you are my Delight."

1:9
Mt 3:13–17
Lk 3:21, 22
Jn 1:32–34
1:11
Mt 3:17
Lk 3:22

1:7 *I am not even worthy to be his slave,* literally, "Whose shoes I am not worthy to unloose." **1:8** *with water,* or "in water." The Greek word is not clear on this controversial point. *with God's Holy Spirit,* or "in God's Holy Spirit"; the Greek is not clear.

1:5 The purpose of John's preaching was to prepare people to accept Jesus as God's Son. When John challenged the people to confess sin individually, he signaled the start of a new approach to having a relationship with God.

Is change needed in your life before you can hear and understand Jesus' message? People have to admit that they need forgiveness before they can accept forgiveness; thus true repentance must come before a person can have true faith in Jesus Christ. To prepare to receive Christ, we must repent, denouncing the world's dead-end attractions, sinful temptations, and harmful attitudes.

1:6 John's clothes were not the latest style of his day. He dressed much like the prophet Elijah (2 Kings 1:8) in order to distinguish himself from the religious leaders whose long-flowing robes reflected their great pride in their position. John's striking appearance reflected his striking message.

1:7, 8 Although John was regarded as the first genuine prophet in 400 years, Jesus the Messiah would be infinitely greater than he. John was pointing out how insignificant he was compared to the One who was coming. He was not even worthy of doing the most menial tasks for him, like untying his shoes. What John began, Jesus finished. What John prepared, Jesus fulfilled.

1:8 John said Jesus would baptize with the Holy Spirit; Jesus would send the Holy Spirit to live within each believer. John's baptism with water prepared a person to receive Christ's message. It demonstrated humility and willingness to turn from sin. This was the *beginning* of the spiritual process.

When Jesus baptizes with the Holy Spirit, however, the entire person will be transformed by the Holy Spirit's power. This baptism is the result of the completed work of Jesus.

1:9 If John's baptism was only for the repentance of sin, why was Jesus baptized? While even the greatest prophets (Isaiah, Jeremiah, Ezekiel) had to confess their sinfulness and need for repentance, Jesus didn't need to admit sin—he was sinless. Although it was unnecessary, Jesus was baptized for the following reasons: (1) to acknowledge his commitment to his mission to bring the message of salvation to all people; (2) to demonstrate that

JESUS BEGINS HIS MINISTRY
When Jesus came from his home in Nazareth to begin his ministry, he first took two steps in preparation—baptism by John in the Jordan River, and temptation by Satan in the rough wilderness of Judea. After the temptations, Jesus returned to Galilee, setting up his home base in Capernaum.

he truly was God's Son and that God approved and endorsed his mission; (3) to officially begin his public ministry (John 1:31–34); (4) to identify with our humanness and sin; (5) to give us an example to follow. John's baptism was different than Christian baptism in the church.

1:9 Jesus grew up in Nazareth, where he had lived since he was a young boy (Matthew 2:22, 23). Nazareth was a small town in Galilee, located about halfway between the Sea of Galilee and the Mediterranean Sea. The city was despised and avoided by many Jews because it was an outpost for Roman troops in the region. Devout Jews hated the Romans for making them pay taxes and for showing little respect for God.

1:10, 11 The Holy Spirit descended dovelike upon Jesus and the voice from heaven proclaimed the Father's approval of Jesus as his divine Son. That Jesus is God's divine Son is the foundation for all we read about Jesus in the Gospels. Here we see all three members of the Trinity together—God the Father, God the Son, and God the Holy Spirit. God is three distinct "persons" in one divine being.

JOHN THE BAPTIST

There's no getting around it—John the Baptist was unique. He wore odd clothes and ate strange food and preached an unusual message to the Judeans who went into the wastelands to see him.

But John did not aim at uniqueness for its own sake. Instead, he aimed at obedience. He knew he had a specific role to play in the world—announcing the coming of the Savior—and he put all his energies into this task. Luke tells us that John was in the desert when God's word of direction came to him. John was ready and waiting. The angel who had announced John's birth to Zacharias had made it clear this child was to be a Nazirite—one set apart for God's service. John remained faithful to that description.

This wild-looking man had no power or position in the Jewish political system, but he spoke with almost irresistible authority. People were moved by his words because he spoke the truth, challenging them to turn from their sins and baptizing them as a symbol of their repentance. They responded by the hundreds. But even as people crowded to him, he pointed beyond himself, never forgetting that his main role was to announce the coming of the Savior.

The words of truth that moved many to repentance goaded others to resistance and resentment. John even challenged King Herod to admit his sin. Herodias, the woman whom Herod had married illegally, decided to get rid of this desert preacher. Although she was able to have him killed, she was not able to stop his message. The One John had announced was already on the move. John had accomplished his mission.

God has given each of us a purpose for living, and we can trust him to guide us. John did not have the complete Bible as we know it today. Yet he focused his life on the truth he knew from the available Old Testament Scriptures. Likewise we can discover in God's Word the truths he wants us to know. And as these truths work in us, others will be drawn to him. God can use you unlike anyone else. Let him know your willingness to follow him today.

Strengths and accomplishments:
• The God-appointed messenger to announce the arrival of Jesus
• A preacher whose theme was repentance
• A fearless confronter
• Known for his remarkable life-style
• Uncompromising

Weaknesses and mistakes:
• Momentary doubt about Jesus' identity

Lessons from his life:
• God does not guarantee an easy or safe life to those who serve him
• Doing what God desires is the greatest possible life-investment
• Standing for the truth is more important than life itself

Key verse:
"Truly, of all men ever born, none shines more brightly than John the Baptist. And yet, even the lesser lights in the Kingdom of Heaven will be greater than he is!" (Matthew 11:11).

Vital statistics:
Where: Judea
Occupation: Prophet
Relatives: Father, Zacharias. Mother, Elizabeth. Distant cousin, Jesus.
Contemporaries: Herod, Herodias

John's story is told in all four Gospels. His coming was predicted in Isaiah 40:3 and Malachi 4:5ff; and he is mentioned in Acts 1:5, 22; 10:37; 11:16; 13:24, 25; 18:25; 19:3, 4.

Satan tempts Jesus in the wilderness
(18/Matthew 4:1–11; Luke 4:1–13)

^{12, 13} Immediately the Holy Spirit urged Jesus into the desert. There, for forty days, alone except for desert animals, he was subjected to Satan's temptations to sin. And afterwards the angels came and cared for him.

1:12
Mt 4:1–11
Lk 4:1–13
1 Tim 3:16

B. MESSAGE AND MINISTRY OF JESUS, THE SERVANT (1:14—13:37)

Mark tells us dramatic, action-packed stories. He gives us the most vivid account of Christ's activities. He features facts and actions, rather than teachings. Seeing Jesus live his life is the perfect example of how we should live our lives today.

1. Jesus' ministry in Galilee

Jesus preaches in Galilee
(30/Matthew 4:12–17; Luke 4:14, 15; John 4:43–45)

¹⁴ Later on, after John was arrested by King Herod, Jesus went to Galilee to preach God's Good News.

¹⁵ "At last the time has come!" he announced. "God's Kingdom is near! Turn from your sins and act on this glorious news!"

1:14
Mt 4:12, 17, 23
Lk 4:14, 15
1:15
Dan 2:44; 9:24, 25
Gal 4:4
Eph 1:10
1 Tim 2:6
Tit 1:3

Four fishermen follow Jesus
(33/Matthew 4:18–22)

¹⁶ One day as Jesus was walking along the shores of the Sea of Galilee, he saw Simon and his brother Andrew fishing with nets, for they were commercial fishermen.

¹⁷ Jesus called out to them, "Come, follow me! And I will make you fishermen for the souls of men!" ¹⁸ At once they left their nets and went along with him.

¹⁹ A little farther up the beach, he saw Zebedee's sons, James and John, in a boat mending their nets. ²⁰ He called them too, and immediately they left their father Zebedee in the boat with the hired men and went with him.

1:16
Mt 4:18–22
Lk 5:1–11
Jn 1:35–42
1:18
Mt 19:27

1:12, 13 *afterwards,* implied in parallel passages. **1:14** *King Herod,* implied.

1:12, 13 Jesus left the crowds and went into the desert, where he was tempted by Satan. Temptation is bad for us only when we give in. Times of inner testing should not be hated and resented, because through them our character can be strengthed and God can teach us valuable lessons. When you face temptation and must deal with his temptations and the turmoil he brings, remember Jesus. He used God's Word against Satan and won. You can do the same.

1:12, 13 Satan is an angel who rebelled against God. He is real, not symbolic, and is constantly working against God and those who obey him. He tempted Eve in the garden and persuaded her to sin; he tempted Jesus in the wilderness and did not persuade him to fall. To be tempted is not a sin. Tempting others or giving in to temptation is sin. For a more detailed account of Jesus' temptation read Matthew 4:1–11.

1:12, 13 To identify fully with human beings, Jesus had to endure Satan's temptations. Because Jesus faced temptations and overcame them, he can assist us in two important ways: (1) as an example of how to face temptation without sinning, and (2) as our helper who knows just what we need, since he went through the same experience. (See Hebrews 4:15, 16 for more on Jesus and temptation.)

1:14, 15 What is God's Good News? These first words spoken by Jesus in Mark give the core of his teaching: that the long-awaited Messiah has come to begin God's personal reign on earth. Most of the people who heard this message were oppressed, poor, and without hope. Jesus' words were good news because they offered freedom, blessings, and promise.

1:16 Fishing was a major industry around the Sea of Galilee. Fishing with nets was the most common method. Capernaum, which became Jesus' new home (Matthew 4:12, 13), was the largest of more than 30 fishing villages around the sea at that time.

1:16-20 We often assume that Jesus' disciples were great men of faith from the first time they met Jesus. But they had to grow in their faith just as all believers do (Mark 14:48–50, 66–72; John 14:1–9; 20:26–29). This is apparently not the only time Jesus called Peter, James, and John to follow him (see Luke 5:1–11 and John 1:35–42 for two other times). It took time for Jesus' call and his message to get through, but the important thing is this: though the disciples had much growing to do, they *followed.*

Jesus teaches with great authority
(34/Luke 4:31–37)

1:21
Lk 4:31–41

1:22
Mt 7:28

21 Jesus and his companions now arrived at the town of Capernaum and on Saturday morning went into the Jewish place of worship—the synagogue—where he preached. 22 The congregation was surprised at his sermon because he spoke as an authority, and didn't try to prove his points by quoting others—quite unlike what they were used to hearing!

1:24
Mt 8:29
Jn 6:69
Acts 3:14
Jas 2:19

23 A man possessed by a demon was present and began shouting, 24 "Why are you bothering us, Jesus of Nazareth—have you come to destroy us demons? I know who you are—the holy Son of God!"

1:26
Mk 9:20

25 Jesus curtly commanded the demon to say no more and to come out of the man. 26 At that the evil spirit screamed and convulsed the man violently and left him. 27 Amazement gripped the audience and they began discussing what had happened.

"What sort of new religion is this?" they asked excitedly. "Why, even evil spirits obey his orders!"

28 The news of what he had done spread quickly through that entire area of Galilee.

Jesus heals Peter's mother-in-law and many others
(35/Matthew 8:14–17; Luke 4:38–41)

1:29
Mt 8:14–17
Lk 4:18–31

29, 30 Then, leaving the synagogue, he and his disciples went over to Simon and Andrew's home, where they found Simon's mother-in-law sick in bed with a high fever. They told Jesus about her right away. 31 He went to her bedside, and as he took her by the hand and helped her to sit up, the fever suddenly left, and she got up and prepared dinner for them!

1:32
Mt 8:16, 17
Lk 4:40, 41

32, 33 By sunset the courtyard was filled with the sick and demon-possessed,

1:22 *Quite unlike what they were used to hearing,* literally, "not as the scribes."

1:21 Because the Temple in Jerusalem was too far for many Jews to travel to for regular worship, many towns had synagogues which served both as places of worship and as schools. Beginning in the days of Ezra, about 450 B.C., a group of ten Jewish families could start up a synagogue. There, during the week, Jewish boys were taught the Old Testament law and Jewish religion. Girls could not attend. Each Saturday, the Sabbath, the Jewish men would gather to listen to a rabbi teach from God's Word. Because there was no permanent rabbi or teacher, it was customary for the synagogue leader to ask visiting teachers to speak. This is why Jesus often spoke in the towns he visited.

1:21 Jesus had recently moved to Capernaum from Nazareth (Matthew 4:12, 13). Capernaum was a thriving city with great wealth as well as great sin and decadence. Because it was the headquarters for many Roman troops, pagan influences from all over the Roman Empire were everywhere. This was an ideal place for Jesus to challenge both Jews and non-Jews with the Good News of God's kingdom.

1:22 The Jewish teachers often quoted from well-known rabbis to give their words more authority. But Jesus didn't need to do that. Since he was God, he knew exactly what the Scriptures said and meant. He was the ultimate authority.

1:23 What are demons? Demons are evil spirits who are ruled by Satan. They work to tempt people to sin. They were not created by Satan, because God is the Creator of all; rather they are fallen angels who joined Satan in his rebellion. In their degenerate state they can cause a person to become mute, deaf, blind, or insane. But in every case where they confronted Jesus, they lost their power. Thus God limits what they can do; they can do nothing without his permission. During Jesus' life on earth demons were allowed to be very active to show once and for all Christ's power and authority over them.

1:23ff Many psychologists dismiss accounts of demon possession as a primitive way to describe mental illness. Clearly, however, a demon controlled the man described here. Mark emphasizes Jesus' conflict with evil powers to show his superiority over them, and so he records many stories about Jesus casting out demons. Jesus didn't have to conduct an elaborate exorcism ritual. His word was enough to send out the demons.

1:23, 24 The demon knew at once that Jesus was the Son of God. Mark, by including this event in his Gospel, was establishing Jesus' credentials, showing that even the underworld recognized Jesus as the Messiah.

1:29-31 Each Gospel writer had a slightly different perspective as he wrote; thus the comparable stories in the gospels often highlight different details. In Matthew, Jesus touched the woman's hand. In Mark, he helped her sit up. In Luke, he spoke to the fever and it left her. The accounts do not conflict. Each writer chose to emphasize different details of the story in order to highlight a certain characteristic of Jesus.

1:32, 33 The people came to Jesus in the evening as the sun was setting. This was the Sabbath (verse 21), their day of rest, lasting from sunset Friday to sunset Saturday. The Jewish leaders had proclaimed that it was against the law to be healed on the Sabbath (Matthew 12:10; Luke 13:14). The people didn't want to break this law or the Jewish law that prohibited traveling on the Sabbath, so they waited until sunset. After the sun went down, the crowds were free to find Jesus so he could heal them.

brought to him for healing; and a huge crowd of people from all over the city of Capernaum gathered outside the door to watch. ³⁴ So Jesus healed great numbers of sick folk that evening and ordered many demons to come out of their victims. (But he refused to allow the demons to speak, because they knew who he was.)

1:34
Mk 3:12
Acts 16:16, 17

Jesus preaches throughout Galilee
(36/Matthew 4:23–25; Luke 4:42–44)

³⁵ The next morning he was up long before daybreak and went out alone into the wilderness to pray.

1:35
Lk 4:42–44
Heb 5:7

³⁶, ³⁷ Later, Simon and the others went out to find him, and told him, "Everyone is asking for you."

³⁸ But he replied, "We must go on to other towns as well, and give my message to them too, for that is why I came."

1:38
Isa 61:1

³⁹ So he traveled throughout the province of Galilee, preaching in the synagogues and releasing many from the power of demons.

1:39
Mt 4:23

Jesus heals a man with leprosy
(38/Matthew 8:1–4; Luke 5:12–16)

⁴⁰ Once a leper came and knelt in front of him and begged to be healed. "If you want to, you can make me well again," he pled.

1:40
Jer 32:17
Mt 8:2–4
Lk 5:12–16

⁴¹ And Jesus, moved with pity, touched him and said, "I want to! Be healed!" ⁴² Immediately the leprosy was gone—the man was healed!

1:41
Heb 2:17; 4:15

⁴³, ⁴⁴ Jesus then told him sternly, "Go and be examined immediately by the Jewish priest. Don't stop to speak to anyone along the way. Take along the offering prescribed by Moses for a leper who is healed, so that everyone will have proof that you are well again."

1:44
Lev 14:1–32

⁴⁵ But as the man went on his way he began to shout the good news that he was healed; as a result, such throngs soon surrounded Jesus that he couldn't publicly enter a city anywhere, but had to stay out in the barren wastelands. And people from everywhere came to him there.

1:45
Mk 3:7; 6:31–34

1:34 Why didn't Jesus want the demons to reveal who he was? (1) By commanding the demons to remain silent, he proved his authority and power over them. (2) Jesus wanted the people to believe he was the Messiah because of what he said and did, not because of the demons' words. (3) He wanted to reveal his identity as the Messiah according to his timetable, not according to Satan's timetable. Satan wanted the people to follow Jesus based on his popularity, not because he was the Son of God.

1:35 Jesus took time to pray. Finding time to pray is not easy, but prayer is the vital link between us and God. Like Jesus, we must find time away from others to talk with God, even if we have to get up before daybreak to do it!

1:36, 37 "The others" probably refers to the disciples Jesus had already called—Andrew, James, John, and perhaps Philip and Nathanael.

1:39 The Romans divided the land of Israel into three separate regions: Galilee, Samaria, and Judea. Galilee was the northernmost region, an area about 60 miles long and 30 miles wide. Jesus spent much of his ministry in this area, an ideal place for him to teach because there were over 250 towns concentrated in this small area. Jesus didn't have far to walk to spread his great message.

1:40, 41 Jewish leaders declared lepers unclean. This meant they were unfit to participate in any religious or social activity. Because their law said that contact with any unclean person made them unclean too, some even threw rocks at lepers to keep them at a safe distance. But Jesus touched this leper.

The real value of a person is inside, not outside. Although a person's body may be diseased or deformed, the person inside is no less valuable to God. No person is too disgusting for his touch. In a sense, we are all lepers, because we have all been deformed by the ugliness of sin. But God, by sending his Son Jesus, has touched us, giving us the opportunity to be healed. When you feel repulsed by someone, stop and remember how God feels about that person—and about you.

1:43, 44 The Old Testament laws about lepers are found in Leviticus 13, 14. When a leper was cured, he or she had to go to a priest to be examined. Then the leper was to give an offering of thanks at the Temple. Jesus adhered to these laws by sending the man to the priest, demonstrating his complete regard for God's law. Sending a healed leper to a priest was also a way to verify Jesus' great miracle to the community.

Jesus heals a paralyzed man
(39/Matthew 9:1–8; Luke 5:17–26)

2:1
Mt 9:1–8
Lk 5:17–26

2:2
Eph 2:17
Heb 2:3

2 Several days later he returned to Capernaum, and the news of his arrival spread quickly through the city. ²Soon the house where he was staying was so packed with visitors that there wasn't room for a single person more, not even outside the door. And he preached the Word to them. ³Four men arrived carrying a paralyzed man on a stretcher. ⁴They couldn't get to Jesus through the crowd, so they dug through the clay roof above his head and lowered the sick man on his stretcher, right down in front of Jesus.

2:5
Ps 103:3

⁵When Jesus saw how strongly they believed that he would help, Jesus said to the sick man, "Son, your sins are forgiven!"

2:7
Ps 130:4
Isa 43:25
Rom 8:33

2:8
Heb 4:13

⁶But some of the Jewish religious leaders said to themselves as they sat there, ⁷"What? This is blasphemy! Does he think he is God? For only God can forgive sins."

⁸Jesus could read their minds and said to them at once, "Why does this bother you? ⁹, ¹⁰, ¹¹I, the Messiah, have the authority on earth to forgive sins. But talk is cheap—anybody could say that. So I'll prove it to you by healing this man." Then, turning to the paralyzed man, he commanded, "Pick up your stretcher and go on home, for you are healed!"

2:12
Mt 9:33

¹²The man jumped up, took the stretcher, and pushed his way through the stunned onlookers! Then how they praised God. "We've never seen anything like this before!" they all exclaimed.

Jesus eats with sinners at Matthew's house
(40/Matthew 9:9–13; Luke 5:27–32)

2:13
Mt 9:9–13
Lk 5:27–32

¹³Then Jesus went out to the seashore again, and preached to the crowds that gathered around him. ¹⁴As he was walking up the beach he saw Levi, the son of Alphaeus, sitting at his tax collection booth. "Come with me," Jesus told him. "Come be my disciple."

And Levi jumped to his feet and went along.

2:4 *right down in front of Jesus,* implied. **2:6** *religious leaders,* literally, "scribes." **2:9-11** *Messiah,* literally, "Son of Man."

2:3 The paralyzed man's need moved his friends to action, and they brought him to Jesus. When you recognize someone's need, do you act? Many people have physical and spiritual needs you can meet, either by yourself or with others who are also concerned. Human need moved these four men; let it also move you to compassionate action.

2:4 Houses in Bible times were built of stone. They had flat roofs made of mud mixed with straw. Outside stairways led to the roofs. These friends, therefore, could have carried the lame man up the outside stairs to the roof. They then could easily have taken apart the mud and straw mixture to make a hole through which to lower their friend to Jesus.

2:7 Instead of saying to the paralyzed man, "You are healed," Jesus said, "Your sins are forgiven." To the Jewish leaders this was blasphemy, claiming to do something only God could do. According to Jewish law, this sin deserved death (Leviticus 24:15, 16). The religious leaders understood correctly that Jesus was claiming to be the Messiah, but their judgment of him was wrong. Jesus was not blaspheming, because his claim was true. Jesus is God, and he proved his claim by healing the paralyzed man (verses 9–11).

2:9-11 This is the first time in Mark that Jesus calls himself the "Son of Man" (see mg.). The title *Son of Man* emphasizes that Jesus is fully human, while *Son of God* (see, for example, John 20:31) emphasizes that he is fully God. As God's Son, Jesus has the authority to forgive sin.

As a man, he can identify with our deepest needs and sufferings and help us overcome sin.

2:14 Levi is another name for the disciple Matthew, who wrote the Gospel of Matthew. See Matthew's Profile in Matthew 9 for more information.

2:14 Capernaum was a key military center for Roman troops as well as a thriving business community. Several major highways intersected in Capernaum, with merchants passing through from as far away as Egypt to the south and Mesopotamia to the north.

Matthew was a Jew who was appointed by the Romans to be the area's tax collector. He collected taxes from the citizens as well as from the merchants passing through town. Tax collectors were expected to take a commission on the taxes they collected, but most of them overcharged and vastly enriched themselves. Tax collectors were hated by the Jews because of their reputation for cheating and their support of Rome. The Jews also hated to think that some of the money collected went to support pagan religions and temples.

2:14, 15 The day that Levi met Jesus, he held a meeting at his house to introduce others to him. He didn't waste any time starting to witness! Some people feel that new believers should wait for time, maturity, or training before they start telling others about Jesus. But like Levi, new believers can tell others about their faith right away with whatever knowledge, skill, or experience they already have.

¹⁵ That night Levi invited his fellow tax collectors and many other notorious sinners to be his dinner guests so that they could meet Jesus and his disciples. (There were many men of this type among the crowds that followed him.) ¹⁶ But when some of the Jewish religious leaders saw him eating with these men of ill repute, they said to his disciples, "How can he stand it, to eat with such scum?"

¹⁷ When Jesus heard what they were saying, he told them, "Sick people need the doctor, not healthy ones! I haven't come to tell good people to repent, but the bad ones."

2:16
Isa 65:5

2:17
Mt 18:11
Lk 19:9, 10
1 Tim 1:15

2:16 *religious leaders,* literally, "the scribes of the Pharisees."

Name and Selected References	Description	Agreement with Jesus	Disagreement with Jesus	PROMINENT JEWISH RELIGIOUS AND POLITICAL GROUPS
PHARISEES Matthew 5:20 Matthew 23:1–36 Luke 6:2 Luke 7:36–47	Strict religious group of Jews, who advocated minute obedience to the Jewish law and traditions. Very influential in the synagogues.	Respect for the Law, belief in the resurrection of the dead, committed to obeying God's will.	Rejected Jesus' claim to be Messiah because he did not follow all their traditions and associated with notoriously wicked people.	
SADDUCEES Matthew 3:7 Matthew 16:11, 12 Mark 12:18	Wealthy, upper class Jewish priestly party. Rejected the authority of the Bible beyond the five books of Moses. Profited from business in the Temple. They, along with the Pharisees, were the two major parties of the Jewish Supreme Court.	Showed great respect for the five books of Moses, as well as the sanctity of the Temple.	Denied the resurrection of the dead. Thought the Temple could also be used as a place to transact business.	
SCRIBES Matthew 7:29 Mark 2:6 Mark 2:16	Professional interpreters of the Law—who especially emphasized the traditions. Many scribes were Pharisees.	Respect for the Law. Committed to obeying God.	Denied Jesus' authority to reinterpret the Law. Rejected Jesus as Messiah because he did not obey all of their traditions.	
HERODIANS Matthew 22:16 Mark 3:6 Mark 12:13	A Jewish political party of King Herod's supporters.	Unknown. In the Gospels they tried to trap Jesus with questions and plotted to kill him.	Afraid of Jesus causing political instability. They saw Jesus as a threat to their political future, at a time when they were trying to regain from Rome some of their lost political power.	
ZEALOTS Matthews 10:4 Luke 6:15 Acts 1:14	A fiercely dedicated group of Jewish patriots determined to end Roman rule in Israel.	Concerned about the future of Israel. Believed in the Messiah but did not recognize Jesus as the One sent by God.	Believed that the Messiah must be a political leader who would deliver Israel from Roman occupation.	
ESSENES none	Jewish monastic group practicing ritual and ceremonial purity as well as personal holiness.	Emphasized justice, honesty, commitment.	Fulfilling detailed ceremonial rituals was an essential aspect of righteousness.	

2:16, 17 "Such scum," the self-righteous Pharisees said, describing the people with whom Jesus ate. But Jesus associated with sinners because he loved them and because he knew they needed to hear what he had to say. He spent time with whoever needed or wanted to hear his message—poor, rich, evil, good. We, too, must befriend those who need Christ, even if they do not seem to be ideal companions. Are there people you have been neglecting because of their reputation? They may be the ones who most need to see and hear the message of Christ's love from you.

Religious leaders ask Jesus about fasting
(41/Matthew 9:14–17; Luke 5:33–39)

2:18
Mt 9:14–17
Lk 5:33–39

2:19
Isa 54:5
Jn 3:29
Rev 19:7

2:22
Gal 3:1–3

18 John's disciples and the Jewish leaders sometimes fasted, that is, went without food as part of their religion. One day some people came to Jesus and asked why his disciples didn't do this too.

19 Jesus replied, "Do friends of the bridegroom refuse to eat at the wedding feast? Should they be sad while he is with them? 20 But some day he will be taken away from them, and then they will mourn. 21 [Besides, going without food is part of the old way of doing things.] It is like patching an old garment with unshrunk cloth! What happens? The patch pulls away and leaves the hole worse than before. 22 You know better than to put new wine into old wineskins. They would burst. The wine would be spilled out and the wineskins ruined. New wine needs fresh wineskins."

The disciples pick wheat on the Sabbath
(45/Matthew 12:1–8; Luke 6:1–5)

2:23
Deut 23:25
Mt 12:1–8
Lk 6:1–5

2:25
Ex 25:30
29:32, 33
Lev 24:9
1 Sam 21:1–6

2:27
Ex 23:12
Deut 5:14
Jn 7:21–24

23 Another time, on a Sabbath day as Jesus and his disciples were walking through the fields, the disciples were breaking off heads of wheat and eating the grain.

24 Some of the Jewish religious leaders said to Jesus, "They shouldn't be doing that! It's against our laws to work by harvesting grain on the Sabbath."

25, 26 But Jesus replied, "Didn't you ever hear about the time King David and his companions were hungry, and he went into the house of God—Abiathar was High Priest then—and they ate the special bread only priests were allowed to eat? That was against the law too. 27 But the Sabbath was

2:21 *way of doing things,* implied. **2:23** *eating the grain,* implied. **2:25, 26** *special bread,* literally "shewbread."

2:18ff John had two purposes: to cause people to repent of their sin, and to prepare them for Christ's coming. This was a time of sober reflection, and so it included fasting, an outward sign of humility and regret for sin. Fasting empties the body of food; repentance empties our lives of sin. Jesus' disciples did not need to fast to prepare for his coming, because he was with them. Jesus did not condemn fasting however. He himself fasted for 40 days (Matthew 4:2). Nevertheless, he emphasized fasting with the right motives. The Pharisees fasted twice a week to show how holy they were. Jesus explained that if people fast only to impress others, they have missed the purpose of fasting.

2:19 Jesus compared himself to a bridegroom because in the Old Testament, the term *bride* is often used for Israel and *bridegroom* for the God who loves her (Jeremiah 2:2; Ezekiel 16:8–14; Matthew 25:1–14).

2:21, 22 A wineskin was a goatskin sewed together at the edges to form a watertight bag. New wine, expanding as it aged, stretched the wineskin. New wine, therefore, could not be put into a wineskin that had already been stretched. The old rigid skin would burst.

The Pharisees had become rigid like old wineskins. They could not accept faith in Jesus which cannot be contained or limited by man-made ideas or rules. Your heart, like a wineskin, can become rigid and prevent you from accepting the new life that Christ offers. Keep your heart open and pliable to accept the life-changing truths of Jesus' message.

2:23 Jesus and his disciples were not stealing when they were picking grain in the field. Leviticus 19:9, 10 and Deuteronomy 23:25 say that Jewish farmers were to leave the corners and edges of their fields unharvested so that the grain could be picked by travelers and by the poor. Just as walking on a sidewalk is not trespassing on private property, eating grain at the edge of a field was not stealing.

2:24 God's law said that crops should not be harvested on the Sabbath (Exodus 34:21). This law prevented farmers from becoming greedy and ignoring God on the Sabbath. It also protected laborers from being overworked. The Pharisees interpreted the action of Jesus and his disciples—picking off the heads of grain and rubbing them in their hands—as harvesting; and so they judged Jesus a lawbreaker. But Jesus and the disciples clearly were not picking the wheat for personal gain; they were simply looking for something to eat. The Pharisees focused so intently on the specific rule that they missed its true intent.

2:24 The Jewish religious leaders were so caught up in their man-made laws that they lost sight of what was good and right. Jesus implied in Mark 3:4 that the Sabbath is a day to do good. God provided the Sabbath as a day of rest and worship, but he didn't mean that concern for rest should keep us from lifting a finger to help others. Don't allow your Sabbath to become a time of selfish indulgence.

2:27, 28 Jesus used the example of King David to point out how ridiculous the Pharisees' accusations were. Jesus said that God created the Sabbath for our benefit, not his own. God derives no benefit from having us rest on the Sabbath, but we are restored both physically and spiritually when we take time to rest and focus on God. For the Pharisees, Sabbath laws had become more important than the reason for the Sabbath. Both David and Jesus understood that the true intent of God's law is to promote love for God and for others. Don't blindly keep a law without looking carefully at the reasons for the law. The spirit of the law is usually more important than the letter.

made to benefit man, and not man to benefit the Sabbath. ²⁸ And I, the Messiah, have authority even to decide what men can do on Sabbath days!"

2:28
Col 2:16, 17

Jesus heals a man's hand on the Sabbath
(46/Matthew 12:9–14; Luke 6:6–11)

3 While in Capernaum Jesus went over to the synagogue again, and noticed a man there with a deformed hand. ² Since it was the Sabbath, Jesus' enemies watched him closely. Would he heal the man's hand? If he did, they planned to arrest him! ³ Jesus asked the man to come and stand in front of the congregation. ⁴ Then turning to his enemies he asked, "Is it all right to do kind deeds on Sabbath days? Or is this a day for doing harm? Is it a day to save lives or to destroy them?" But they wouldn't answer him. ⁵ Looking around at them angrily, for he was deeply disturbed by their indifference to human need, he said to the man, "Reach out your hand." He did, and instantly his hand was healed!

3:1
Mt 12:9–16
Lk 6:6–11, 17–19

⁶ At once the Pharisees went away and met with the Herodians to discuss plans for killing Jesus.

3:6
Mt 22:16

Large crowds follow Jesus
(47/Matthew 12:15–21)

⁷, ⁸ Meanwhile, Jesus and his disciples withdrew to the beach, followed by a huge crowd from all over Galilee, Judea, Jerusalem, Idumea, from beyond the Jordan River, and even from as far away as Tyre and Sidon. For the news about his miracles had spread far and wide and vast numbers came to see him for themselves.

3:7
Mt 12:15–21
Lk 6:17–19

⁹ He instructed his disciples to bring around a boat and to have it standing ready to rescue him in case he was crowded off the beach. ¹⁰ For there had been many healings that day and as a result great numbers of sick people were crowding around him, trying to touch him. ¹¹ And whenever those possessed by demons caught sight of him they

3:11
Mk 1:24, 25, 34
Lk 4:41
Acts 16:16, 17

2:28 *the Messiah,* literally, "the Son of Man."

3:2 Already the Jewish leaders had turned against Jesus. They were jealous of his popularity, his miracles, and his speaking authority. They valued their status in the community and their opportunity for personal gain so much that they lost sight of their goal as religious leaders—to point people toward God. Of all people, they should have recognized the Messiah, but they refused to acknowledge him because they were not willing to give up their treasured position and power. When Jesus exposed their true attitudes, he became their enemy instead of their Messiah, and they began looking for ways to turn the people against him to stop his growing popularity.

3:4 Jesus did a good deed, but the Pharisees accused him of breaking their law that said medical attention could be given to no one on the Sabbath except in matters of life and death. Ironically, the Pharisees were accusing Jesus of breaking the Sabbath by healing someone, while at the same time they were plotting murder.

3:5 Jesus was angry about the Pharisees' uncaring attitudes. Anger itself is not wrong. It depends on what makes us angry and what we do with our anger. Too often we express our anger in selfish and harmful ways. By contrast, Jesus expressed his anger by correcting a problem—healing the man's hand. Use your anger to find constructive solutions rather than to add to the problem by tearing people down.

3:6 The Pharisees were a Jewish religious group who zealously followed Old Testament law as well as their own religious traditions. They were highly respected in the community, but they hated Jesus because he challenged their proud attitudes and dishonorable motives.

The Herodians were a Jewish political party that hoped to restore Herod the Great's line to the throne. Jesus was a threat to them as well because he challenged their political ambitions. The Pharisees and Herodians, normally enemies, joined forces against Jesus because he exposed them for what they were and undermined their power and reputations.

3:7, 8 While Jesus was drawing fire from the religious leaders, he was gaining great popularity among the people. Some were curious, some sought healing, some wanted evidence to use against him, and others wanted to know if he truly was the Messiah. Most of them only dimly guessed the real scope of what was happening among them. Today crowds still follow Jesus, and they come for the same variety of reasons. What is your primary reason for following Jesus?

3:11 The demons knew that Jesus was God's Son, but they refused to turn from their evil purpose. Knowing about Jesus, or even believing that he is God's Son, does not guarantee salvation. You must also want to follow and obey him (James 2:17).

would fall down before him shrieking, "You are the Son of God!" [12] But he strictly warned them not to make him known.

Jesus selects the twelve disciples
(48/Luke 6:12–16)

3:13
Mt 10:2–4
Lk 6:12–16
3:14
Lk 9:1
3:16
Jn 1:42

[13] Afterwards he went up into the hills and summoned certain ones he chose, inviting them to come and join him there; and they did. [14, 15] Then he selected twelve of them to be his regular companions and to go out to preach and to cast out demons. [16–19] These are the names of the twelve he chose: Simon (he renamed him "Peter"), James and John (the sons of Zebedee, but Jesus called them "Sons of Thunder"), Andrew, Philip, Bartholomew, Matthew, Thomas, James (the son of Alphaeus), Thaddaeus, Simon (a member of a political party advocating violent overthrow of the Roman government), Judas Iscariot (who later betrayed him).

Religious leaders accuse Jesus of being Satan
(74/Matthew 12:22–37)

3:20
Mk 6:31

[20] When he returned to the house where he was staying, the crowds began to gather again, and soon it was so full of visitors that he couldn't even find time to eat. [21] When his friends heard what was happening they came to try to take him home with them.

"He's out of his mind," they said.

3:22
Mt 9:34; 10:25
12:22–32
Lk 11:14–23
Jn 8:48, 52
10:20

[22] But the Jewish teachers of religion who had arrived from Jerusalem said, "His trouble is that he's possessed by Satan, king of demons. That's why demons obey him."

[23] Jesus summoned these men and asked them (using proverbs they all understood), "How can Satan cast out Satan? [24] A kingdom divided against itself will collapse. [25] A home filled with strife and division destroys itself.

3:26
Mt 4:10
3:27
Isa 49:24, 25

[26] And if Satan is fighting against himself, how can he accomplish anything? He would never survive. [27] [Satan must be bound before his demons are cast

3:27 *cast out,* implied.

3:12 Jesus warned the demons not to make him known as Messiah because they would be reinforcing a popular misconception. The huge crowds were looking for a political and military leader who would free them from Rome's control, and they thought the Messiah predicted by the Old Testament prophets would be this kind of man. Jesus wanted to teach the people about the kind of Messiah he really was—far different from their expectations. His kingdom is spiritual. It begins, not with the overthrow of governments, but with the overthrow of sin in people's hearts.

3:14 Jesus was surrounded by followers, from whom he chose twelve to be his regular companions. He did not choose these twelve because of their faith, because their faith faltered. He didn't choose them because of their talent and ability, because no one stood out with unusual ability. The disciples represented a wide range of backgrounds and life experiences, but apparently they had no more leadership potential than those who were not chosen. The one characteristic they all shared was their willingness to obey and follow Jesus. After Jesus' ascension, they were filled with the Holy Spirit and carried out special roles in the growth of the early church. We should not disqualify ourselves from service to Christ because we do not have the right credentials. Being a good disciple is simply a matter of following Jesus with a willing heart.

3:14–16 Why did Jesus choose twelve men? The number twelve corresponds to the twelve tribes of Israel (Matthew

19:28), showing the continuity between the old religious system and the new, based on Jesus' message. Many people followed Jesus, but these twelve received the most intense training. We see the impact of these men throughout the rest of the New Testament.

3:21 With the crowds pressing in on him, Jesus didn't even take time to eat. Because of this, his friends and family came from Nazareth to take him home (verses 31, 32), thinking he had gone "over the edge" as a religious fanatic. They were concerned for him, but they missed the point of his ministry. Even those who were closest to Jesus were slow to understand his true identity.

3:22–26 The Pharisees could not deny Jesus' miracles and supernatural power. They refused to believe that his power was from God, however, because then they would have had to accept him as the Messiah. Their pride would not let them do that. So in an attempt to destroy his popularity among the people, they accused him of having power from Satan. We can see from Jesus' reply in verses 23–26 that the argument of the Jewish leaders didn't make sense.

3:27 Although God permits Satan to work in our world, God is still in control. Jesus, because he is God, has power over Satan; he is able to cast out demons and end their terrible work in people's lives. One day Satan will be bound forever, never again to do his evil work in the world (Revelation 20:10).

Name	Occupation	Outstanding Characteristics	Major Events in His Life
SIMON PETER (son of John)	Fisherman	Impulsive; later—bold in preaching Jesus	One of three in core group of disciples; recognized Jesus as the Messiah; denied Christ and repented; preached Pentecost sermon; a leader of the Jerusalem church; baptized Gentiles; wrote 1 and 2 Peter.
JAMES, son of Zebedee. He and his brother John were called the "Sons of Thunder"	Fisherman	Ambitious, short-tempered, judgmental, deeply committed to Jesus	Also in core group; he and his brother John asked Jesus for places of honor in his kingdom; wanted to command fire to fall on a Samaritan village; first disciple to be martyred.
JOHN (son of Zebedee), James' brother, and "the disciple Jesus loved"	Fisherman	Ambitious, judgmental, later—very loving	Third disciple in core group; asked Jesus for a place of honor in his kingdom; wanted to call down fire on a Samaritan village; a leader of the Jerusalem church; wrote the Gospel of John and 1, 2, 3 John and Revelation.
ANDREW (Peter's brother)	Fisherman	Eager to bring others to Jesus	Accepted John the Baptist's testimony about Jesus; told Peter about Jesus; he and Philip told Jesus that Greeks wanted to see him.
PHILIP	Fisherman	Questioning attitude	Told Nathanael about Jesus; wondered how Jesus could feed the 5,000; asked Jesus to show his followers God the Father; he and Andrew told Jesus that Greeks wanted to see him.
BARTHOLOMEW (Nathanael)	Unknown	Honesty and straight-forwardness	Initially rejected Jesus because he was from Nazareth but acknowledged Jesus as the "Son of God" and "King of Israel" when they met.
MATTHEW (Levi)	Tax collector	Despised outcast because of his dishonest career	Abandoned his corrupt (and financially profitable) way of life to follow Jesus; invited Jesus to a party with his notorious friends; wrote the Gospel of Matthew.
THOMAS (the Twin)	Unknown	Courage and doubt	Suggested the disciples go with Jesus to Bethany—even if it meant death; asked Jesus about where he was going; refused to believe Jesus was risen until he would see Jesus alive and touch his wounds.
JAMES (son of Alphaeus)	Unknown	Unknown	Became one of Jesus' disciples.
THADDAEUS (Judas, son of James)	Unknown	Unknown	Asked Jesus why he would reveal himself to his followers and not to the world.
SIMON THE ZEALOT	Unknown	Fierce patriotism	Became a disciple of Jesus.
JUDAS ISCARIOT	Unknown	Treacherous and greedy	Became one of Jesus' disciples; betrayed Jesus; killed himself.

Jesus' faithful disciples were ordinary men who became extraordinary because of Jesus Christ. Despite their confusion and misunderstanding during his lifetime, they became powerful witnesses to his resurrection. Their lives were transformed by God's power. The story of Jesus' disciples does not end with the Gospels. It continues in the book of Acts and many of the epistles.

DISCIPLES

What Jesus Said about Him	*A Key Lesson from His Life*	*Selected References*
Named him Peter, "a rock"; called him "Satan" when he urged Jesus to reject the Cross; said he would become a fisherman of men's souls; he received revelation from God; he would deny Jesus; he would later be crucified for his faith.	Christians falter at times; but when they return to Jesus, he forgives them and strengthens their faith.	Matthew 4:18–20 Mark 8:29–33 Luke 22:31–34 John 21:15–19 Acts 2:14–41, 10:1—11:18
Called James and John "Sons of Thunder"; said they would fish for the souls of men; they would drink the cup Jesus drank; they did not understand their own hearts.	Christians must be willing to die for Jesus.	Mark 3:17 Mark 10:35–40 Luke 9:52–56 Acts 12:1, 2
Called James and John "Sons of Thunder"; said he would fish for the souls of men; would drink the cup Jesus drank; did not understand his own heart; would take care of Jesus' mother after his death.	The transforming power of the love of Christ is available to all.	Mark 1:19 Mark 10:35–40 Luke 9:52–56 John 19:26, 27 John 21:20–24
Said he would become a fisherman of men's souls.	Christians are to tell other people about Jesus.	Matthew 4:18–20 John 1:35–42; 6:8, 9 John 12:20–22
Asked if Philip realized that to know and see him was to know and see the Father.	God uses our questions to teach us.	Matthew 10:3 John 1:43–46; 6:2–7 John 12:20–22; 14:8–11
Called him "an honest man" and "a true son of Israel."	Jesus respects honesty in people—even if they challenge him because of it.	Mark 3:18 John 1:45–51 John 21:1–13
Called him to be a disciple.	Christianity is not for people who think they're already good; it is for people who know they've failed and want help.	Matthew 9:9–13 Mark 2:15–17 Luke 5:27–32
Said Thomas believed because he actually saw Jesus after the resurrection.	Even when Christians experience serious doubts, Jesus reaches out to them to restore their faith.	Matthew 10:3 John 14:5; 20:24–29 John 21:1–13
Unknown	Unknown	Matthew 10:3 Mark 3:18 Luke 6:15
Unknown	Christians follow Jesus because they believe in him; they do not always understand the details of God's plan.	Matthew 10:3 Mark 3:18 John 14:22
Unknown	If we are willing to give up our plans for the future, we can participate in Jesus' plans.	Matthew 10:4 Mark 3:18 Luke 6:15
Called him "a devil"; said he would betray Jesus.	It is not enough to be familiar with Jesus' teachings. Jesus' true followers love and obey him.	Matthew 26:20–25 Luke 22:47, 48 John 12:4–8

out], just as a strong man must be tied up before his house can be ransacked and his property robbed.

28 "I solemnly declare that any sin of man can be forgiven, even blasphemy against me; 29 but blasphemy against the Holy Spirit can never be forgiven. It is an eternal sin."

30 He told them this because they were saying he did his miracles by Satan's power [instead of acknowledging it was by the Holy Spirit's power].

3:29
Lk 12:10
1 Jn 5:16

Jesus describes his true family
(76/Matthew 12:46–50; Luke 8:19–21)

31, 32 Now his mother and brothers arrived at the crowded house where he was teaching, and they sent word for him to come out and talk with them. "Your mother and brothers are outside and want to see you," he was told.

33 He replied, "Who is my mother? Who are my brothers?" 34 Looking at those around him he said, "These are my mother and brothers! 35 Anyone who does God's will is my brother, and my sister, and my mother."

3:31
Mt 12:46–50 13:55
Mk 6:3
Lk 8:19–21
Jn 7:3–5

3:34
Rom 8:29
Heb 2:11

3:35
Jn 7:16, 17

Jesus tells the parable of the four soils
(77/Matthew 13:1–9; Luke 8:4–8)

4 Once again an immense crowd gathered around him on the beach as he was teaching, so he got into a boat and sat down and talked from there. 2 His usual method of teaching was to tell the people stories. One of them went like this:

3 "Listen! A farmer decided to sow some grain. As he scattered it across his field, 4 some of it fell on a path, and the birds came and picked it off the hard ground and ate it. 5, 6 Some fell on thin soil with underlying rock. It grew up quickly enough, but soon wilted beneath the hot sun and died because the roots had no nourishment in the shallow soil. 7 Other seeds fell among thorns that shot up and crowded the young plants so that they produced no grain. 8 But some of the seeds fell into good soil and yielded thirty times as much as he had planted—some of it even sixty or a hundred times as much! 9 If you have ears, listen!"

4:1
Mt 13:1–23
Lk 8:4–15

4:9
Mk 4:23

3:30 instead of acknowledging it was by the Holy Spirit's power, implied.

3:28, 29 Christians sometimes wonder if they have committed this sin of blaspheming the Holy Spirit. This is not a sin about which Christians need worry; it is a heart-attitude of unbelief and unrepentance. Deliberate, ongoing rejection of the work of the Holy Spirit is blasphemy because it is rejecting God himself. The religious leaders accused Jesus of blasphemy, but ironically they were the guilty ones when they looked him in the face and called him Satan.

3:31–35 Jesus' mother was Mary (Luke 1:30, 31) and his brothers were probably the other children Mary and Joseph had after Jesus. Many Christians, however, believe the ancient tradition that Jesus was Mary's only child. If this is true, the "brothers" were possibly cousins (cousins were often called brothers in those days). Jesus' family did not yet fully understand his ministry, as can be seen in verse 21. Jesus explained that our spiritual family forms relationships that are ultimately more important and longer lasting than those formed in our physical families.

3:33–35 God's family is open and doesn't exclude anyone. Although Jesus cared for his mother and brothers, he also cared for all those who loved him. Jesus did not show partiality; he allowed everyone the privilege of obeying God and becoming part of his family. He shows us how to relate to other believers in a new way. In our increasingly computerized, impersonal world, warm relationships among members of God's family take on major importance. The church can give loving, personalized care that many people find nowhere else.

4:2 Jesus taught the people by telling stories, often called parables. A parable uses familiar scenes to explain deeper spiritual truth. This method of teaching compels the listener to think. It conceals the truth from those who are too stubborn or prejudiced to hear what is being taught. Most parables have one main point, so we must be careful not to go beyond what Jesus intended to teach.

4:3 Seed was planted, or sowed, by hand. As the farmer walked across the field, he threw handfuls of seed onto the ground from a large bag slung across his shoulders. The plants did not grow in neat rows as with today's machine planting. No matter how skillful he may have been, no farmer could keep all his seed from falling on the path or among rocks and thorns or from being carried off by the wind. He threw the seed liberally, however, and enough fell on good ground to ensure the harvest.

4:9 We hear with our ears, but there is a deeper kind of listening with the mind and heart that is necessary in order to gain spiritual understanding from Jesus' words. Some people in the crowd were looking for evidence to use against Jesus; others truly wanted to learn and grow. Jesus' words were for the honest seekers.

Jesus explains the parable of the four soils
(78/Matthew 13:10–23; Luke 8:9–18)

4:11, 12
Isa 6:9; 44:18
Jer 5:21
Jn 12:39, 40
Acts 28:26, 27
Rom 11:8
1 Cor 2:10

10 Afterwards, when he was alone with the twelve and with his other disciples, they asked him, "What does your story mean?"

11, 12 He replied, "You are permitted to know some truths about the kingdom of God that are hidden to those outside the kingdom:

'Though they see and hear, they will not understand or turn to God, or be forgiven for their sins.'

13 But if you can't understand *this* simple illustration, what will you do about all the others I am going to tell?

4:14
Eph 3:8
Jas 1:18
1 Pet 1:23–25

4:15
2 Cor 4:4
1 Pet 5:8

14 "The farmer I talked about is anyone who brings God's message to others, trying to plant good seed within their lives. 15 The hard pathway, where some of the seed fell, represents the hard hearts of some of those who hear God's message; Satan comes at once to try to make them forget it. 16 The rocky soil represents the hearts of those who hear the message with joy, 17 but, like young plants in such soil, their roots don't go very deep, and though at first they get along fine, as soon as persecution begins, they wilt.

4:19
Prov 23:4, 5
Lk 18:24
1 Tim 6:9, 10, 17
1 Jn 2:15, 16

18 "The thorny ground represents the hearts of people who listen to the Good News and receive it, 19 but all too quickly the attractions of this world and the delights of wealth, and the search for success and lure of nice things come in and crowd out God's message from their hearts, so that no crop is produced.

4:20
Jn 15:5

4:21
Mt 5:15
Lk 8:16–18
11:33

4:22
Mt 10:26
Lk 12:2

4:23
Mt 11:15; 13:43

4:25
Mt 13:12; 25:29
Lk 6:38; 19:26
2 Cor 9:6

20 "But the good soil represents the hearts of those who truly accept God's message and produce a plentiful harvest for God—thirty, sixty, or even a hundred times as much as was planted in their hearts. 21 Then he asked them, "When someone lights a lamp, does he put a box over it to shut out the light? Of course not! The light couldn't be seen or used. A lamp is placed on a stand to shine and be useful.

22 "All that is now hidden will someday come to light. 23 If you have ears, listen! 24 And be sure to put into practice what you hear. The more you do this, the more you will understand what I tell you. 25 To him who has shall be given; from him who has not shall be taken away even what he has.

4:11, 12 Some people do not understand God's truth because they are not ready for it. God reveals truth to people who will act on it, who will make it evident in their lives. When you talk with people about God, be aware that they will not understand if they are not yet ready. Be patient, taking every chance to tell them more of the truth about God and praying that the Holy Spirit will open their minds and hearts, making them ready to receive the truth and act on it.

4:14–20 The four soils represent four different ways people respond to God's Word. Usually we think that Jesus was talking about four different kinds of people. But he may also have been talking about (1) different times or phases in a person's life, or (2) how we willingly receive God's message in some areas of our life and resist it in others. For example, you may be open to God about your future, but closed concerning how you spend your money. You may respond like good soil to God's demand for worship, but like rocky soil to his demand to give to

those in need. We must strive to be like good soil in every area of our life at all times.

4:21 If a lamp doesn't help people see, it is useless. Does your life show other people how to find God and how to live for him? If not, ask what "boxes" have shut out your light. Complacency, resentment, stubbornness of heart, or disobedience could be "boxes" that keep God's light from shining through you to others.

4:21–24 The light of Jesus' truth is revealed to us, not hidden. But we may not be able to see or to use all of that truth right now. Only as we put God's teachings into practice will we understand and see more of the truth. The truth is clear, but our ability to understand is imperfect. As we obey, we will sharpen our vision and increase our understanding (James 1:22–25).

4:25 This phrase simply means we are responsible to use well what we have. It doesn't matter how much we have but what we do with it.

Jesus tells the parable of the growing seed
(79)

²⁶"Here is another story illustrating what the Kingdom of God is like:

"A farmer sowed his field, ²⁷and went away, and as the days went by, the seeds grew and grew without his help. ²⁸For the soil made the seeds grow. First a leaf-blade pushed through, and later the wheat-heads formed and finally the grain ripened, ²⁹and then the farmer came at once with his sickle and harvested it."

Jesus tells the parable of the mustard seed
(81/Matthew 13:31, 32)

³⁰Jesus asked, "How can I describe the Kingdom of God? What story shall I use to illustrate it? ³¹,³²It is like a tiny mustard seed! Though this is one of the smallest of seeds, yet it grows to become one of the largest of plants, with long branches where birds can build their nests and be sheltered."

³³He used many such illustrations to teach the people as much as they were ready to understand. ³⁴In fact, he taught only by illustrations in his public teaching, but afterwards, when he was alone with his disciples, he would explain his meaning to them.

Jesus calms the storm
(87/Matthew 8:23-27; Luke 8:22-25)

³⁵As evening fell, Jesus said to his disciples, "Let's cross to the other side of the lake." ³⁶So they took him just as he was and started out, leaving the crowds behind (though other boats followed). ³⁷But soon a terrible storm arose. High waves began to break into the boat until it was nearly full of water and about to sink. ³⁸Jesus was asleep at the back of the boat with his head on a cushion. Frantically they wakened him, shouting, "Teacher, don't you even care that we are all about to drown?"

³⁹Then he rebuked the wind and said to the sea, "Quiet down!" And the wind fell, and there was a great calm!

⁴⁰And he asked them, "Why were you so fearful? Don't you even yet have confidence in me?"

⁴¹And they were filled with awe and said among themselves, "Who is this man, that even the winds and seas obey him?"

4:33 *as much as they were ready to understand,* literally, "as they were able to hear."

Marginal references:

4:26, 27
1 Cor 3:6, 7

4:28, 29
Mt 9:37, 38
Lk 10:2
Jn 4:35
1 Cor 15:36-38
Rev 14:15

4:30
Mt 13:31, 32
Lk 13:18, 19

4:31, 32
Gen 1:11, 12
Ps 104:12
Ezek 17:22, 23;
37:6
Dan 4:12, 21
Acts 2:41; 4:4; 5:14

4:33
Mt 13:34, 35

4:34
Jn 10:6; 16:25

4:35
Mt 8:23-27
Lk 8:22-25

4:39
Job 38:11
Ps 65:7; 89:9 93:4

4:41
Ps 33:8, 9

4:26-29 This parable about the Kingdom of God, recorded only by Mark, reveals that spiritual growth is a continual, gradual process that is finally consummated in a harvest of spiritual maturity. We can understand the process of spiritual growth by comparing it to the slow but certain growth of a plant.

4:30-32 Jesus used this parable to explain that although Christianity had very small beginnings, it would grow into a worldwide community of believers. When you feel alone in your stand for Christ, realize that God is building a worldwide kingdom. He has faithful followers in every part of the world, and your faith, no matter how small, can join with that of others to accomplish great things.

4:33, 34 Jesus adapted his methods to his audience's ability and desire to understand. He didn't speak in parables to confuse people, but to challenge sincere seekers to discover the true meaning of his words. Much of Jesus' teaching was against hypocrisy and impure motives, characteristics of the religious leaders. Had Jesus spoken against the leaders directly, his public ministry would have been hampered. Those who truly listened to Jesus knew what he was talking about.

4:37, 38 The Sea of Galilee is 680 feet below sea level, and it is surrounded by hills. Winds blowing across the land intensify close to the sea, causing violent and unexpected storms. The disciples were seasoned fishermen who had spent their lives fishing on this huge lake, but in this storm they panicked.

4:38-40 The disciples panicked because the storm threatened to destroy them all, and Jesus seemed unaware and unconcerned. Theirs was a physical storm, but storms come in other forms too. Think about the storms in your life—the situations that cause you great anxiety. Whatever your difficulty, you have two options. You can worry and assume that Jesus no longer cares, or you can resist fear, putting your trust in him. When you feel like panicking, confess your need for God and then trust him to care for you.

4:41 The disciples lived with Jesus, but they underestimated him. They did not see that his power

Jesus sends the demons into a herd of pigs
(88/Matthew 8:28–34; Luke 8:26–39)

5:1
Mt 8:28–34
Lk 8:26–39

5 When they arrived at the other side of the lake a demon-possessed man ran out from a graveyard, just as Jesus was climbing from the boat. ³,⁴This man lived among the gravestones, and had such strength that whenever he was put into handcuffs and shackles—as he often was—he snapped the handcuffs from his wrists and smashed the shackles and walked away. No one was strong enough to control him. ⁵All day long and through the night he would wander among the tombs and in the wild hills, screaming and cutting himself with sharp pieces of stone.

THE TOUCH OF JESUS
What kind of people did Jesus associate with? Whom did he consider important enough to touch? Here we see many of the people Jesus came to know. Some reached out to him; he reached out to them all. Regardless of how great or unknown, rich or poor, young or old, sinner or saint— Jesus cares equally for all. No person is beyond the loving touch of Jesus.

Jesus Talked with . . .	*Reference*
A despised tax collector	Matthew 9:9
An insane hermit	Mark 5:1–15
The Roman governor	Mark 15:1–15
A young boy	Mark 9:17–27
A prominent religious leader	John 3:1–21
A homemaker	Luke 10:38–42
A lawyer	Matthew 22:34, 35
A criminal	Luke 23:40–43
A synagogue ruler	Mark 5:22
A fisherman	Matthew 4:18–20
A king	Luke 23:7–11
A poor widow	Luke 7:11–17; 21:1–4
A Roman army captain	Luke 7:1–10
A group of children	Mark 10:13–16
A prophet	Matthew 3
An adulterous woman	John 8:1–11
The Jewish Supreme Court	Luke 22:66–71
A sick old woman	Mark 5:25–34
A rich man	Mark 10:17–23
A blind beggar	Mark 10:46
Jewish political leaders	Mark 12:13
A group of women	Luke 8:2, 3
The High Priest	Matthew 26:62–68
An outcast with leprosy	Luke 17:11–19
A city official	John 4:46–53
A young girl	Mark 5:41, 42
A traitor	John 13:1–3
A helpless and paralyzed man	Mark 2:1–12
An angry mob of soldiers and police	John 18:3–9
A woman from a foreign land	Mark 7:25–30
A doubting follower	John 20:24–29
An enemy who hated him	Acts 9:1–9

---

applied to their own situation. We've had 20 centuries of Jesus with us, and yet we, like the disciples, underestimate his power to handle crises in our lives. The disciples did not yet know enough about Jesus. We cannot claim the same excuse.

5:1 Although we cannot be sure why demon possession occurs, we know that it uses the body in a destructive way to distort and destroy man's relationship with God and likeness to him. Even today, demons are dangerous, powerful, and destructive. While it is important to recognize their evil activity so we can stay away from them, we must avoid any curiosity about or involvement with demonic forces or the occult (Deuteronomy 18:10–12). If we resist the devil and his influences, he will flee from us (James 4:7).

HEALING A DEMON POSSESSED MAN
From Capernaum, Jesus and his disciples crossed the Sea of Galilee. A storm blew up unexpectedly, but Jesus calmed it. Landing in the country of the Gadarenes, Jesus sent demons out of a man and into swine that plunged over the steep bank into the sea.

⁶When Jesus was still far out on the water, the man had seen him and had run to meet him, and fell down before him.

⁷,⁸Then Jesus spoke to the demon within the man and said, "Come out, you evil spirit."

It gave a terrible scream, shrieking, "What are you going to do to me, Jesus, Son of the Most High God? For God's sake, don't torture me!"

⁹"What is your name?" Jesus asked, and the demon replied, "Legion, for there are many of us here within this man."

¹⁰Then the demons begged him again and again not to send them to some distant land.

¹¹Now as it happened there was a huge herd of hogs rooting around on the hill above the lake. ¹²"Send us into those hogs," the demons begged.

¹³And Jesus gave them permission. Then the evil spirits came out of the man and entered the hogs, and the entire herd plunged down the steep hillside into the lake and drowned.

¹⁴The herdsmen fled to the nearby towns and countryside, spreading the news as they ran. Everyone rushed out to see for themselves. ¹⁵And a large crowd soon gathered where Jesus was; but as they saw the man sitting there, fully clothed and perfectly sane, they were frightened. ¹⁶Those who saw what happened were telling everyone about it, ¹⁷and the crowd began pleading with Jesus to go away and leave them alone! ¹⁸So he got back into the boat. The man who had been possessed by the demons begged Jesus to let him go along. ¹⁹But Jesus said no.

"Go home to your friends," he told him, "and tell them what wonderful things God has done for you; and how merciful he has been."

²⁰So the man started off to visit the Ten Towns of that region and began to tell everyone about the great things Jesus had done for him; and they were awestruck by his story.

5:20 to visit the Ten Towns, or, "to visit Decapolis."

5:7, 8 Lk 8:28; Acts 16:17; Heb 7:1
5:11 Deut 14:8; Isa 65:4
5:13 Job 1:12; 2:6; 12:16; Mt 28:18; Lk 4:36; Col 2:10; Heb 2:8
5:15 1 Jn 3:8
5:17 Job 21:14; 22:17; Lk 5:8
5:18 Ps 116:12
5:20 Isa 63:7; 116:16; 1 Tim 1:13, 14

5:9 The demon said its name was "Legion." A legion was the largest unit of the Roman army, consisting of 3,000 to 6,000 soldiers. Obviously this man was possessed by not one but many demons.

5:10 Mark often highlights the supernatural struggle between Jesus and Satan. The demons' goal was to control the humans they inhabited; Jesus' goal was to give people freedom from sin and Satan's control. The demons knew they had no power over Jesus, so when they saw him, they begged not to be sent to a distant land (called the Bottomless Pit in Luke 8:31). Jesus granted their request (verse 13) but ended their destructive work in people. He could have sent them to hell, but he did not because the time for judgment had not yet come. In the end, of course, all demons will be sent into eternal fire (Matthew 25:41).

5:11 According to Old Testament law (Leviticus 11:7), pigs were "unclean" animals. This meant they could not be eaten or even touched by a Jew. This incident took place southeast of the Sea of Galilee in the Gerasene country, a Gentile region, which explains how a herd of pigs could be involved.

5:17 After such a wonderful miracle of saving a man's life, why did the people want Jesus to leave? The people asked Jesus to leave because they were afraid of his supernatural power, a power that seemed uncontrollable. They may have also feared that Jesus would continue to eliminate their source of livelihood by destroying their pigs. They would rather give up Jesus than their source of income and security.

5:19 Jesus told this man to tell his friends about the miraculous healing. Most of the time, Jesus urged those he healed to keep quiet. Why the change? Here are possible answers: (1) The demon-possessed man had been alone and unable to speak. Telling others what Jesus did for him would prove that he was healed. (2) This was mainly a Gentile and pagan area, so Jesus was not expecting great crowds to follow him or religious leaders to hinder him. (3) By sending the man away with this good news, Jesus was expanding his ministry to people who were not Jews.

5:19, 20 This man had been demon possessed but now was a living example of Jesus' power. He wanted to go with Jesus, but Jesus told him to go home and share his story there. If you have experienced Jesus' power, you too are a living example. Are you, like this man, enthusiastic about sharing the good news with those around you? Just as we would tell others about a doctor who cured a physical disease, we should tell about Christ who cures our sin.

5:20 The region of the Ten Towns, called the Decapolis in Greek, was located southeast of the Sea of Galilee. Ten cities, each with its own independent government, formed an alliance for protection and to increase trade. These cities had been settled several centuries earlier by Greek traders and immigrants. Although Jews also lived in the area, they were not in the majority. Many people from these ten towns followed Jesus (Matthew 4:25).

Jesus heals a bleeding woman and restores a girl to life
(89/Matthew 9:18–26; Luke 8:40–56)

5:21
Mt 9:1, 18–26
Lk 8:40–56

21 When Jesus had gone across by boat to the other side of the lake, a vast crowd gathered around him on the shore.

22 The leader of the local synagogue, whose name was Jairus, came and fell down before him, 23 pleading with him to heal his little daughter.

5:23
Mk 6:5; 7:32; 8:23;
16:18
Lk 4:40; 13:13
Acts 6:6; 9:17; 28:8

"She is at the point of death," he said in desperation. "Please come and place your hands on her and make her live."

24 Jesus went with him, and the crowd thronged behind. 25 In the crowd was a woman who had been sick for twelve years with a hemorrhage. 26 She had suffered much from many doctors through the years and had become poor from paying them, and was no better but, in fact, was worse. 27 She had heard all about the wonderful miracles Jesus did, and that is why she came up behind him through the crowd and touched his clothes.

5:27
Mk 3:10
Acts 19:11, 12

28 For she thought to herself, "If I can just touch his clothing, I will be healed." 29 And sure enough, as soon as she had touched him, the bleeding stopped and she knew she was well!

5:30
Lk 6:19

30 Jesus realized at once that healing power had gone out from him, so he turned around in the crowd and asked, "Who touched my clothes?"

31 His disciples said to him, "All this crowd pressing around you, and you ask who touched you?"

32 But he kept on looking around to see who it was who had done it. 33 Then the frightened woman, trembling at the realization of what had happened to her, came and fell at his feet and told him what she had done. 34 And he said to her, "Daughter, your faith has made you well; go in peace, healed of your disease."

5:34
Mk 10:52
Lk 7:50; 17:19
18:42
Acts 14:9

35 While he was still talking to her, messengers arrived from Jairus' home with the news that it was too late—his daughter was dead and there was no point in Jesus' coming now. 36 But Jesus ignored their comments and said to Jairus, "Don't be afraid. Just trust me."

5:36
Jn 11:25, 40

37 Then Jesus halted the crowd and wouldn't let anyone go on with him to Jairus' home except Peter and James and John. 38 When they arrived, Jesus saw that all was in great confusion, with unrestrained weeping and wailing. 39 He went inside and spoke to the people.

5:39
Jn 11:11

"Why all this weeping and commotion?" he asked. "The child isn't dead; she is only asleep!"

5:40
Acts 9:40

40 They laughed at him in bitter derision, but he told them all to leave, and

---

5:22 Jesus recrossed the Sea of Galilee, probably landing at Capernaum. Jairus was the elected ruler of the local synagogue. He was responsible for supervising worship, running the weekly school, and caring for the building. Many synagogue rulers had close ties to the Pharisees. It is likely, therefore, that some synagogue rulers had been pressured not to support Jesus. For Jairus to bow before Jesus was a significant and perhaps daring act of respect and worship.

5:25-34 This woman had an incurable condition causing her to bleed constantly. This may have been a menstrual or uterine disorder which would have made her ritually unclean (Leviticus 15:25-27) and excluded her from most social contact with other Jews. She desperately wanted Jesus to heal her, but she knew her bleeding would cause Jesus to be "unclean" under Jewish law if she touched him. Still, she reached out by faith and was healed. Sometimes we feel our problems will keep us from God. But he is always ready to help, and we should never allow our fear to keep us from approaching him.

5:32-34 Jesus was not angry with this woman for touching him. Jesus knew she had touched him, but he

stopped and asked who did it in order to teach her something about faith. Although she was healed when she touched him, Jesus said her faith caused the cure. Genuine faith involves action. Faith that isn't put into action is no faith at all.

5:36 Jairus' crisis made him feel confused, afraid, and without hope. Jesus' words to Jairus in the midst of crisis speak to us as well: "Don't be afraid. Just trust me." In Jesus' mind, there was both hope and promise. The next time you feel as Jairus did, remember to see your problem from Jesus' point of view. He is the source of all hope and promise.

5:38 Loud mourning and crying was customary at a person's death. Lack of it was the ultimate disgrace and disrespect. Some people, usually women, made mourning a profession, and were paid by the dead person's family to weep over the body. On the day of death, the body was carried through the streets, followed by the mourners and others who felt obligated to join the procession.

5:39, 40 The mourners began to mock Jesus when he said, "She isn't dead; she is only asleep." The girl was

taking the little girl's father and mother and his three disciples, he went into the room where she was lying.

⁴¹, ⁴² Taking her by the hand he said to her, "Get up, little girl!" (She was twelve years old.) And she jumped up and walked around! Her parents just couldn't get over it. ⁴³ Jesus instructed them very earnestly not to tell what had happened, and told them to give her something to eat.

5:41, 42
Ps 33:9
Lk 7:14

5:43
Mt 12:16; 17:9
Mk 3:12; 5:19
Lk 5:14

The people of Nazareth refuse to believe
(91/Matthew 13:53–58)

6 Soon afterwards he left that section of the country and returned with his disciples to Nazareth, his home town. ², ³ The next Sabbath he went to the synagogue to teach, and the people were astonished at his wisdom and his miracles because he was just a local man like themselves.

"He's no better than we are," they said. "He's just a carpenter, Mary's boy, and a brother of James and Joseph, Judas and Simon. And his sisters live right here among us." And they were offended!

⁴ Then Jesus told them, "A prophet is honored everywhere except in his home town and among his relatives and by his own family." ⁵ And because of their unbelief he couldn't do any mighty miracles among them except to place his hands on a few sick people and heal them. ⁶ And he could hardly accept the fact that they wouldn't believe in him.

Then he went out among the villages, teaching.

6:1
Mt 13:53–58
9:35
Lk 4:16, 22, 24

6:2, 3
Ps 69:8
Isa 53:2, 3
Mt 11:6
Jn 6:42

6:4
Jn 4:44

---

dead, but Jesus used the image of sleep to indicate that her condition was temporary and she would be restored. Whether Jesus was talking about her physical or spiritual life doesn't matter. In either case, her life would continue.

Jesus tolerated the crowd's abuse in order to teach an important lesson about maintaining hope and trust in him. Today most of the world laughs at God's claims, which seem ridiculous to them. When you are belittled for expressing faith in Jesus and hope for eternal life, remember that unbelievers don't see from God's perspective. For a clear statement about life after death, see 1 Thessalonians 4:13, 14.

5:41, 42 Jesus not only demonstrated great power; he also showed tremendous compassion. Jesus' power over nature, demons, and death was motivated by compassion—for a demonic man who lived among tombs, for a diseased woman, and for the family of a dead girl. The rabbis of the day considered such people unclean. Polite society avoided them. But Jesus reached out and helped anyone in need.

5:43 Jesus told the girl's parents not to spread the news of the miracle. He wanted the facts to speak for themselves, and the time was not yet right for a major confrontation with the religious leaders. Jesus still had much to accomplish, and he didn't want people following him just to see his miracles.

6:2, 3 Jesus was teaching effectively and wisely, but the people of his hometown saw him as only a carpenter. "He's no better than us—he's just a common laborer," they said. They were offended that others could be impressed by him and follow him. They rejected his authority because he was one of their peers. They thought they knew him, but their preconceived notions made it impossible for them to accept his message. Don't let prejudice blind you to truth. Try to see Jesus for who he really is.

PREACHING IN GALILEE
After returning to his home town, Nazareth, from Capernaum Jesus preached in the villages of Galilee and sent his disciples out to preach as well. After meeting back in Capernaum, they left by boat to rest in a "quieter spot" only to be met by the crowds who followed the boat along the shore.

6:4 Jesus said that a prophet (in other words, a worker for God) is never honored in his hometown. But that doesn't make his work any less important. A person doesn't need to be respected or honored to be useful to God. If friends, neighbors, or family don't respect your Christian work, don't let their rejection keep you from serving God.

6:5 Jesus could have done greater miracles in Nazareth, but he chose not to because of the people's pride and unbelief. The miracles he did had little effect on the people because they did not want to accept his message or believe he was from God. Therefore, Jesus looked elsewhere, seeking those who would respond to his miracles and message.

Jesus sends out the twelve disciples
(93/Matthew 10:1-15; Luke 9:1-6)

6:7
Mt 10:1, 9-14; 11:1
Lk 9:1-6
10:1-11

7 And he called his twelve disciples together and sent them out two by two, with power to cast out demons. 8, 9 He told them to take nothing with them except their walking sticks—no food, no knapsack, no money, not even an extra pair of shoes or a change of clothes.

10 "Stay at one home in each village—don't shift around from house to house while you are there," he said. 11 "And whenever a village won't accept you or listen to you, shake off the dust from your feet as you leave; it is a sign that you have abandoned it to its fate."

6:11
Acts 13:51; 18:6
Heb 10:31

12 So the disciples went out, telling everyone they met to turn from sin. 13 And they cast out many demons, and healed many sick people, anointing them with olive oil.

6:13
Jas 5:14

Herod kills John the Baptist
(95/Matthew 14:1-12; Luke 9:7-9)

6:14
Mt 14:1-12
Lk 9:7-9

14 King Herod soon heard about Jesus, for his miracles were talked about everywhere. The king thought Jesus was John the Baptist come back to life again. So the people were saying, "No wonder he can do such miracles." 15 Others thought Jesus was Elijah the ancient prophet, now returned to life again; still others claimed he was a new prophet like the great ones of the past.

6:15
Mt 16:14

16 "No," Herod said, "it is John, the man I beheaded. He has come back from the dead."

6:17
Lev 18:15, 16 20:21
Lk 3:19
2 Tim 4:2
Heb 13:4

17, 18 For Herod had sent soldiers to arrest and imprison John because he kept saying it was wrong for the king to marry Herodias, his brother Philip's wife. 19 Herodias wanted John killed in revenge, but without Herod's approval she was powerless. 20 And Herod respected John, knowing that he was a good and holy man, and so he kept him under his protection. Herod was disturbed whenever he talked with John, but even so he liked to listen to him.

6:7 The disciples were sent out in pairs. Individually they could have reached more areas of the country, but this was not Christ's plan. One advantage in going out by twos was that they could strengthen and encourage each other, especially when they faced rejection. Our strength comes from God, but he meets many of our needs through our teamwork with others. As you serve him, don't try to go it alone.

6:8, 9 Mark records that the disciples were instructed to take nothing with them *except* walking sticks, while in the Matthew and Luke accounts Jesus told them *not* to take a walking stick. One explanation is that Matthew and Luke were referring to a club used for protection, whereas Mark was talking about a shepherd's crook. In any case, the point in all three accounts is the same—the disciples were to leave at once, without extensive preparation, trusting in God's care rather than in their own resources.

6:11 Pious Jews shook the dust from their feet after passing through Gentile cities or territory to show their separation from Gentile influences and practices. When the disciples shook the dust from their feet after leaving a *Jewish* town, it was a vivid sign that the people had rejected Jesus and his message. Jesus made it clear that the people were responsible for how they responded to the gospel. The disciples were not to blame if the message was rejected, as long as they had faithfully and carefully presented it. We are not responsible when others reject Christ's message of salvation, but we do have the responsibility to share it faithfully with others.

6:15 Herod, along with many others, wondered who Jesus really was. Unable to accept Jesus' claim to be God's Son, many people made up their own explanations for his power and authority. Herod thought Jesus was John the Baptist come back to life, while those who were familiar with the Old Testament thought he was Elijah (Malachi 4:5). Still others believed he was a teaching prophet in the tradition of Moses, Isaiah, or Jeremiah. Today people still have to make up their minds about Jesus. Some think that if they can name what he is—prophet, teacher, good man—they can weaken the power of his claim on their lives. But what they *think* does not change who Jesus *is*.

6:17-19 Palestine was divided into four territories, each ruled by a "tetrarch." Herod Antipas, called King Herod in the Gospels, was ruler over Galilee; his brother Philip ruled over Trachonitus and Idumea. Philip's wife was Herodias, but she left him to marry Herod Antipas. When John confronted the two for committing adultery, Herodias formulated a plot to kill him. Instead of trying to get rid of her sin, she tried to get rid of the one who brought it to public attention. This is exactly what the religious leaders were trying to do to Jesus.

6:20 Herod arrested John the Baptist under pressure from his wife and advisors. Though he respected John's integrity, in the end he had him killed because of pressure from his peers and family. What you do under pressure often shows what you are really like.

²¹ Herodias' chance finally came. It was Herod's birthday and he gave a stag party for his palace aides, army officers, and the leading citizens of Galilee. ²², ²³ Then Herodias' daughter came in and danced before them and greatly pleased them all.

"Ask me for anything you like," the king vowed, "even half of my kingdom, and I will give it to you!"

²⁴ She went out and consulted her mother, who told her, "Ask for John the Baptist's head!"

²⁵ So she hurried back to the king and told him, "I want the head of John the Baptist—right now—on a tray!"

²⁶ Then the king was sorry, but he was embarrassed to break his oath in front of his guests. ²⁷ So he sent one of his bodyguards to the prison to cut off John's head and bring it to him. The soldier killed John in the prison, ²⁸ and brought back his head on a tray, and gave it to the girl and she took it to her mother.

²⁹ When John's disciples heard what had happened, they came for his body and buried it in a tomb.

Jesus feeds five thousand
(96/Matthew 14:13-21; Luke 9:10-17; John 6:1-15)

³⁰ The apostles now returned to Jesus from their tour and told him all they had done and what they had said to the people they visited.

³¹ Then Jesus suggested, "Let's get away from the crowds for a while and rest." For so many people were coming and going that they scarcely had time to eat. ³² So they left by boat for a quieter spot. ³³ But many people saw them leaving and ran on ahead along the shore and met them as they landed. ³⁴ So the usual vast crowd was there as he stepped from the boat; and he had pity on them because they were like sheep without a shepherd, and he taught them many things they needed to know.

³⁵, ³⁶ Late in the afternoon his disciples came to him and said, "Tell the people to go away to the nearby villages and farms and buy themselves some

6:21
Gen 40:20

6:22
Esth 5:3, 6; 7:2

6:27
Rev 6:9

6:29
Acts 8:2

6:30
Mt 14:13-22
Lk 9:10-17
Jn 6:1-15

6:31
Mk 3:20

6:34
Ps 145:8, 9
Isa 61:1
Mt 9:36
Heb 5:1-3

Herod as a leader	Jesus as a leader	
Selfish	Compassionate	**REAL LEADERSHIP** Mark gives us some of the best insights into Jesus' character.
Murderer	Healer	
Immoral	Just and good	
Political opportunist	Servant	
King over small territory	King over all creation	

6:22, 23 As a tetrarch under Roman authority, Herod had no kingdom to give. His offer of half his kingdom was his way to say he would give Herodias' daughter almost anything she wanted. When Herodias asked for John's head, Herod would have been greatly embarrassed in front of his guests if he had denied her request. Words are powerful. Because they can lead to great sin, we should use them with great care.

6:30 Mark uses the word *apostle* only once. *Apostle* means "one sent" as messenger or missionary. The word became an official title for Jesus' twelve disciples after his death and resurrection (Acts 2:14; Ephesians 2:20).

6:31 When the disciples had returned from their mission,

Jesus took them away to rest. Doing God's work is very important, but Jesus recognized that to do God's work effectively requires periodic rest and renewal. Jesus and his disciples, however, did not always find it easy to get the rest they needed!

6:34 This crowd was as pitiful as a flock of sheep without a shepherd. Sheep are easily scattered; without a shepherd they are in grave danger. Jesus knew he was the Shepherd who could teach them what they needed to know and keep them from straying from God. See Psalm 23; Isaiah 61:1; and Ezekiel 34:5-10 for descriptions of the Good Shepherd.

6:37
Num 11:13, 22
2 Kgs 4:43
Mt 15:33
Mk 8:4

food, for there is nothing to eat here in this desolate spot, and it is getting late."

37 But Jesus said, *"You* feed them."

"With what?" they asked. "It would take a fortune to buy food for all this crowd!"

6:37 *It would take a fortune,* literally, "200 denarii," a year's wages.

HEROD ANTIPAS

Most people dislike having their sins pointed out, especially in public. The shame of being exposed is often worse than the guilt brought on by the wrongdoing. Herod Antipas was a man experiencing both guilt and shame.

Herod's ruthless ambition was public knowledge, as was his illegal marriage to his brother's wife, Herodias. One man made Herod's sin a public issue. That man was John the Baptist. John had been preaching in the desert, and thousands flocked to hear him. Apparently John used Herod's life-style as a negative example. Herodias was particularly anxious to have John silenced. As a solution, Herod imprisoned John.

Herod liked John. John was probably one of the few people he met who spoke only the truth. But the truth about his sin was a bitter pill to swallow, and Herod wavered at the point of conflict: he couldn't afford to have John constantly reminding the people of their leader's sinfulness, but he was afraid to have John killed. He put off the choice. Eventually Herodias forced his hand, and John was executed. Of course, this only served to increase Herod's guilt.

Upon hearing about Jesus, Herod immediately identified him with John. He couldn't decide what to do about Jesus. He didn't want to repeat the mistake he had made with John, so he tried to threaten Jesus just before his final journey to Jerusalem. When the two met briefly during Jesus' trial, Jesus would not speak to Herod. Herod had proved himself a poor listener to John, and Jesus had nothing to add to John's words. Herod responded with spite and mocking. Having rejected the messenger, he found it easy to reject the Messiah. For each person, God chooses the best possible ways to reveal himself. He uses his Word, circumstances, our minds, or other people to get our attention. He is persuasive and persistent, but never forces himself on us. To miss or resist God's message, as did Herod, is tragedy. How aware are you of God's attempts to enter your life? Have you welcomed him?

Strengths and accomplishments:
• Built the city of Tiberias and other architectural projects
• Ruled the region of Galilee for the Romans

Weaknesses and mistakes:
• Consumed with his quest for power
• Put off decisions or made wrong ones under pressure
• Divorced his wife to marry the wife of his half-brother, Philip
• Imprisoned John the Baptist and later ordered his execution
• Had a minor part in the execution of Jesus

Lessons from his life:
• A life motivated by ambition is usually characterized by self-destruction
• Opportunities to do good usually come to us in the form of choices to be made

Key verse:
"And Herod respected John, knowing that he was a good and holy man, and so he kept him under his protection. Herod was disturbed whenever he talked to John, but even so he liked to listen to him" (Mark 6:20).

Vital statistics:
Where: Jerusalem
Occupation: Roman tetrarch of the region of Galilee and Perea
Relatives: Father, Herod the Great. Mother, Malthace. First wife, daughter of Aretas IV. Second wife, Herodias.
Contemporaries: John the Baptist, Jesus, Pilate

Herod Antipas' story is told in the Gospels. He is also mentioned in Acts 4:27; 13:1.

6:37 In this chapter different people have examined Jesus' life and ministry: his neighbors and family, Herod the king, and the disciples. Yet none of these appreciate him for who he is. The disciples are still pondering, still unclear, still unbelieving. They do not realize that Jesus can provide for them. They are so preoccupied with the impossibility of the task that they cannot see the possible. Do you let what seems impossible about Christianity keep you from believing?

38 "How much food do we have?" he asked. "Go and find out."

They came back to report that there were five loaves of bread and two fish. 39, 40 Then Jesus told the crowd to sit down, and soon colorful groups of fifty or a hundred each were sitting on the green grass.

41 He took the five loaves and two fish and looking up to heaven, gave thanks for the food. Breaking the loaves into pieces, he gave some of the bread and fish to each disciple to place before the people. 42 And the crowd ate until they could hold no more!

43, 44 There were about 5,000 men there for that meal, and afterwards twelve basketfuls of scraps were picked up off the grass!

6:41
1 Sam 9:13
Mt 26:26
1 Tim 4:4, 5

Jesus walks on water
(97/Matthew 14:22–33; John 6:16–21)

45 Immediately after this Jesus instructed his disciples to get back into the boat and strike out across the lake to Bethsaida, where he would join them later. He himself would stay and tell the crowds good-bye and get them started home.

46 Afterwards he went up into the hills to pray. 47 During the night, as the disciples in their boat were out in the middle of the lake, and he was alone on land, 48 he saw that they were in serious trouble, rowing hard and struggling against the wind and waves.

6:47
Mt 14:23–36
Jn 6:16–21

About three o'clock in the morning he walked out to them on the water. He started past them, 49 but when they saw something walking along beside them they screamed in terror, thinking it was a ghost, 50 for they all saw him.

But he spoke to them at once. "It's all right," he said. "It is I! Don't be afraid." 51 Then he climbed into the boat and the wind stopped!

They just sat there, unable to take it in! 52 For they still didn't realize who he was, even after the miracle the evening before! For they didn't want to believe!

6:52
Mk 16:14

6:52 *For they didn't want to believe,* literally, "For their hearts were hardened."

6:37-42 Jesus asked the disciples to provide food for over 5,000 people. They responded, "With what?" How do you react when you are given an impossible task? A situation that seems impossible with human means is simply an opportunity for God. The disciples did everything they could—they gathered the available food and organized the people into groups. Then, in answer to prayer, God did the impossible. When facing a seemingly impossible task, do what you can and ask God to do the rest. He may see fit to make the impossible happen.

6:49 The disciples were surprised to see Jesus walking beside them on the water. But they should have realized he would help them when they were in trouble. Though they had lost sight of him, he had not lost sight of them. His concern for them overcame their lack of faith. The next time you are in "deep water," remember that Christ knows your struggle and cares for you.

6:50 The disciples were afraid, but Jesus' presence calmed their fears. We all experience fear. Do we try to deal with it ourselves, or do we let Jesus deal with it? In times of fear and uncertainty, it is calming to know that Christ is always with us (Matthew 28:20). To recognize his presence is the antidote for fear.

6:52 The disciples didn't want to believe, perhaps because (1) they couldn't accept the fact that this human named Jesus was really the Son of God; (2) they dared not believe that the Messiah would choose them as his followers—it was too good to be true; (3) they still did not understand the real purpose for Jesus' coming to earth. Their disbelief took the form of misunderstanding.

Even after watching Jesus miraculously feed 5,000 people, they still could not take the final step of faith to believe he was God's Son. If they had, they would not have been amazed that he could walk on water. They did not transfer the truth they already knew about him to their own lives. We read that Jesus walked on the water, and yet we often marvel that he is able to work in our life. We must not only believe these miracles really occurred; we must also transfer the truth to our own life situations.

JESUS WALKS ON THE WATER
After feeding the people who had followed to hear him at Bethsaida-Julias, Jesus sent the people home, sent his disciples by boat toward Bethsaida, and went to pray. The disciples encountered a storm and Jesus walked to them on the water. They landed at Gennesaret.

Jesus heals all who touch him
(98/Matthew 14:34–36)

6:53
Mt 14:34–36
Jn 6:24, 25

6:56
Mk 5:28
Acts 5:15

⁵³ When they arrived at Gennesaret on the other side of the lake they moored the boat, ⁵⁴ and climbed out.

The people standing around there recognized him at once, ⁵⁵ and ran throughout the whole area to spread the news of his arrival, and began carrying sick folks to him on mats and stretchers. ⁵⁶ Wherever he went—in villages and cities, and out on the farms—they laid the sick in the market plazas and streets, and begged him to let them at least touch the fringes of his clothes; and as many as touched him were healed.

Jesus teaches about inner purity
(102/Matthew 15:1–20)

7:1
Mt 15:1–20
7:2
Lk 11:38
7:3
Gal 1:14
Col 2:8

7 One day some Jewish religious leaders arrived from Jerusalem to investigate him, ² and noticed that some of his disciples failed to follow the usual Jewish rituals before eating. ³ (For the Jews, especially the Pharisees, will never eat until they have sprinkled their arms to the elbows, as required by their ancient traditions. ⁴ So when they come home from the market they must always sprinkle themselves in this way before touching any food. This is but one of many examples of laws and regulations they have clung to for centuries, and still follow, such as their ceremony of cleansing for pots, pans and dishes.)

⁵ So the religious leaders asked him, "Why don't your disciples follow our age-old customs? For they eat without first performing the washing ceremony."

7:6, 7
Isa 29:13
Tit 1:16

^{6, 7} Jesus replied, "You bunch of hypocrites! Isaiah the prophet described you very well when he said, 'These people speak very prettily about the Lord

7:3 *sprinkled their arms to the elbows,* literally, "to wash with the fist."

GOSPEL ACCOUNTS FOUND ONLY IN MARK	Section	Topic	Significance
	4:26–29	Story of the growing seeds	We must share the good news of Jesus with other people, but only God makes it grow in their lives.
	7:31–37	Jesus heals a deaf man with a speech impediment	Jesus cares about our physical as well as spiritual needs.
	8:22–26	Jesus heals the blind man of Bethsaida	Jesus is considerate because he makes sure this man's sight is fully restored.

6:53 Gennesaret was a small fertile plain located on the west side of the Sea of Galilee. Capernaum, Jesus' home, sat at the northern edge of this plain.

6:56 Jewish men wore ankle-length robes called tunics. Over the tunic they wore a waist-length vest called a tallith. Four tassels were sewed to the four lower corners of the fringe of the tallith. The people probably expected Jesus' healing power to be released when they touched these tassels on the fringe of his tallith (Matthew 9:20, 21). They may not have realized that it was faith in Jesus, not magical power, that healed them.

7:1ff The religious leaders sent some investigators from their headquarters in Jerusalem to check up on Jesus. They didn't like what they found, however, because Jesus scolded them for keeping the law in order to look holy instead of to honor God. The prophet Isaiah accused the religious leaders of his day for doing the same (Isaiah 29:13). Jesus used Isaiah's words to accuse these men.

7:3, 4 Mark explained these Jewish rituals because he was writing to a non-Jewish audience. Before each meal, devout Jews performed a short ceremony, washing their hands and arms in a specific way. To them, this was a symbol of being cleansed from any contact they might have had with anything considered unclean. Jesus said the Pharisees were wrong in thinking they were acceptable to God because they were clean on the outside.

7:6, 7 Hypocrisy is pretending to be something you are not. Jesus called the Pharisees hypocrites because they worshiped God not because they loved him, but because it was profitable, it made them look holy, and it increased their status in the community. We become hypocrites when we (1) pay more attention to reputation than to character, (2) carefully follow certain religious practices while allowing our hearts to remain distant from God, and (3) emphasize our virtues but others' sins.

but they have no love for him at all. Their worship is a farce, for they claim that God commands the people to obey their petty rules.' How right Isaiah was! ⁸ For you ignore God's specific orders and substitute your own traditions. ⁹ You are simply rejecting God's laws and trampling them under your feet for the sake of tradition.

7:9
Isa 24:4, 5

¹⁰ For instance, Moses gave you this law from God: 'Honor your father and mother.' And he said that anyone who speaks against his father or mother must die. ¹¹ But you say it is perfectly all right for a man to disregard his needy parents, telling them, 'Sorry, I can't help you! For I have given to God what I could have given to you.' ¹², ¹³ And so you break the law of God in order to protect your man-made tradition. And this is only one example. There are many, many others."

7:10
Ex 20:12; 21:17
Lev 20:19
Deut 5:16
Prov 20:20
1 Tim 5:8

7:11
Lev 1:2 (Heb)

¹⁴ Then Jesus called to the crowd to come and hear. "All of you listen," he said, "and try to understand. ¹⁵, ¹⁶ Your souls aren't harmed by what you eat, but by what you think and say!"

7:15
Acts 10:14, 15
1 Cor 8:8
1 Tim 4:4

¹⁷ Then he went into a house to get away from the crowds, and his disciples asked him what he meant by the statement he had just made.

7:17
Mk 2:1, 2; 3:20
9:28

¹⁸ "Don't you understand either?" he asked. "Can't you see that what you eat won't harm your soul? ¹⁹ For food doesn't come in contact with your heart, but only passes through the digestive system." (By saying this he showed that every kind of food is kosher.)

7:19
Lk 11:41
Acts 10:15; 11:9

²⁰ And then he added, "It is the thoughtlife that pollutes. ²¹ For from within, out of men's hearts, come evil thoughts of lust, theft, murder, adultery, ²² wanting what belongs to others, wickedness, deceit, lewdness, envy, slander, pride, and all other folly. ²³ All these vile things come from within; they are what pollute you and make you unfit for God."

7:20
Rom 14:1–12
Col 2:16

7:21
Gal 5:19
Tit 1:15

2. Jesus' ministry beyond Galilee

Jesus sends a demon out of a girl
(103/Matthew 15:21–28)

²⁴ Then he left Galilee and went to the region of Tyre and Sidon, and tried to keep it a secret that he was there, but couldn't. For as usual the news of his arrival spread fast.

7:24
Mt 15:21–28

7:15, 16 Verse 16 is omitted in many of the ancient manuscripts. "If any man has ears to hear, let him hear." *Your souls aren't harmed by what you eat, but by what you think and say,* literally, "what proceeds out of the man defiles the man."

7:8, 9 The Pharisees added hundreds of their own petty rules and regulations to God's holy laws, and then tried to force people to follow them. These men claimed to know God's will in every detail of life. Religious leaders today still try to add rules and regulations to God's Word, causing much confusion among believers. It is idolatry to claim your interpretation of God's Word is as important as God's Word itself. It is especially dangerous to set up non-biblical standards for *others* to follow. Instead, look to Christ for guidance about your own behavior, and let him lead others in the details of their lives.

7:10, 11 The Pharisees used God as an excuse to avoid helping their families, especially their parents. They thought it was more important to put money in the Temple treasury than to help their needy parents, although God's law specifically says to honor fathers and mothers (Exodus 20:12) and to care for those in need (Leviticus 25:35–43). We should give money and time to God, but we must never use God as an excuse to neglect our responsibilities. Helping those in need is one of the most important ways to honor God.

7:18 Do we worry more about what is in our diets than what is in our hearts and minds? As they interpreted the dietary laws (Leviticus 11), the Jews believed they could

be clean before God because of what they *did not* eat. But Jesus pointed out that sin actually begins in the attitudes and intentions of the inner person. He did not downgrade the law, but he paved the way for the change made clear in Acts 10:9–29 when God removed the cultural restrictions regarding food. We are not pure because of outward acts—we become pure on the inside as Christ renews our minds and makes us over in his image.

7:20-23 An evil action begins with a single thought. Our thoughts can pollute us, leading us into sin. Allowing our thoughts to dwell on lust, envy, hate, or revenge will lead to evil actions. Don't be made unfit for God. Instead, "think about things that are pure and lovely, and dwell on the fine good things in others. Think about all you can praise God for and be glad about" (Philippians 4:8).

7:24 Jesus traveled about 50 miles to Tyre and then went to Sidon. These were two port cities on the Mediterranean Sea north of Israel. Both cities had flourishing trade and were very wealthy.

In David's day, Tyre was on friendly terms with Israel (2 Samuel 5:11), but soon afterward the city became known for its wickedness. Its king, Ethbaal, even claimed to be God (Ezekiel 28:1ff). Tyre rejoiced when Jerusalem

7:27
Mt 10:5, 6
Acts 13:46
Rom 9:4
Eph 2:11, 12

7:29
Mt 9:29

7:30
Josh 21:45

7:31
Mt 15:29–31

7:33
Mk 8:23
Jn 9:6

7:34
Isa 35:5, 6
Mt 11:5
Mk 6:41
Jn 11:41; 17:1

7:36
Mk 5:43

²⁵Right away a woman came to him whose little girl was possessed by a demon. She had heard about Jesus and now she came and fell at his feet, ²⁶and pled with him to release her child from the demon's control. (But she was Syrophoenician—a "despised Gentile!")

²⁷Jesus told her, "First I should help my own family—the Jews. It isn't right to take the children's food and throw it to the dogs."

²⁸She replied, "That's true, sir, but even the puppies under the table are given some scraps from the children's plates."

²⁹"Good!" he said, "You have answered well—so well that I have healed your little girl. Go on home, for the demon has left her!"

³⁰And when she arrived home, her little girl was lying quietly in bed, and the demon was gone.

The crowd marvels at Jesus' healings
(104/Matthew 15:29–31)

³¹From Tyre he went to Sidon, then back to the Sea of Galilee by way of the Ten Towns. ³²A deaf man with a speech impediment was brought to him, and everyone begged Jesus to lay his hands on the man and heal him.

³³Jesus led him away from the crowd and put his fingers into the man's ears, then spat and touched the man's tongue with the spittle. ³⁴Then, looking up to heaven, he sighed and commanded, "Open!" ³⁵Instantly the man could hear perfectly and speak plainly!

³⁶Jesus told the crowd not to spread the news, but the more he forbade them, the more they made it known, ³⁷for they were overcome with utter

7:27 *First I should help my own family—the Jews,* literally, "Let the children eat first."

MINISTRY IN PHOENICIA
Jesus' ministry was to all people—first to Jews but also to Gentiles. Jesus took his disciples from Galilee to Tyre and Sidon, large cities in Phoenicia, where he healed a Gentile woman's daughter.

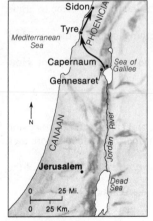

was destroyed in 586 B.C. because without Israel's competition, Tyre's trade and profits would increase. It was into this evil and materialistic culture that Jesus brought his message. It is interesting that he stressed the importance of inner purity just before visiting Tyre.

7:26 This woman is called a Syrophoenician in Mark and a Canaanite in Matthew. Mark's designation refers to her political background. His Roman audience would easily identify her by the part of the Empire that was her home. Matthew's description was designed for his Jewish audience, who remembered the Canaanites as bitter enemies when Israel was settling the Promised Land.

7:27 *Dog* was a term the Jews commonly applied to any Gentiles, because the Jews considered these pagan people no more likely than dogs to receive God's blessing. Jesus, however, was not degrading the woman by using this term, but simply explaining to her God's

plan to present his message first to Jews. The woman did not try to argue. Using Jesus' choice of words, she pointed out that she was willing to be considered a dog as long as she could receive God's blessing for her daughter. Ironically, many Jews would lose God's blessing and salvation because they rejected Jesus. Many Gentiles, whom the Jews considered "dogs," would find salvation because they recognized Jesus.

7:29 This miracle shows that Jesus' power over demons is so great that he doesn't need to be present physically in order to free someone. His power spans any distance.

7:36 Jesus asked the people not to spread the news of this healing because he didn't want to be seen simply as a miracle worker. He didn't want the people to miss his real message.

CONTINUED MINISTRY
After taking a roundabout way back to Galilee through the Ten Towns, Jesus returned to Dalmanutha where Jewish leaders questioned his authority. From there he went to Bethsaida-Julias and on to Caesarea-Philippi. Here he talked with his disciples about his authority and coming events.

amazement. Again and again they said, "Everything he does is wonderful; he even corrects deafness and stammering!"

Jesus feeds four thousand
(105/Matthew 15:32-39)

8 One day about this time as another great crowd gathered, the people ran out of food again. Jesus called his disciples to discuss the situation.

"I pity these people," he said, "for they have been here three days, and have nothing left to eat. ³And if I send them home without feeding them, they will faint along the road! For some of them have come a long distance."

⁴"Are we supposed to find food for them here in the desert?" his disciples scoffed.

⁵"How many loaves of bread do you have?" he asked.

"Seven," they replied. ⁶So he told the crowd to sit down on the ground. Then he took the seven loaves, thanked God for them, broke them into pieces and passed them to his disciples; and the disciples placed them before the people. ⁷A few small fish were found, too, so Jesus also blessed these and told the disciples to serve them.

⁸,⁹And the whole crowd ate until they were full, and afterwards he sent them home. There were about 4,000 people in the crowd that day and when the scraps were picked up after the meal, there were seven very large basketfuls left over!

Religious leaders ask for a sign in the sky
(106/Matthew 16:1-4)

¹⁰Immediately after this he got into a boat with his disciples and came to the region of Dalmanutha.

¹¹When the local Jewish leaders learned of his arrival they came to argue with him.

"Do a miracle for us," they said. "Make something happen in the sky. Then we will believe in you."

¹²He sighed deeply when he heard this and he said, "Certainly not. How many more miracles do you people need?"

Jesus warns against wrong teaching
(107/Matthew 16:5-12)

¹³So he got back into the boat and left them, and crossed to the other side of the lake. ¹⁴But the disciples had forgotten to stock up on food before they left, and had only one loaf of bread in the boat.

¹⁵As they were crossing, Jesus said to them very solemnly, "Beware of the yeast of King Herod and of the Pharisees."

8:11 *Then we will believe in you,* literally, "to test him." **8:12** *How many more miracles do you people need?* literally, "Why does this generation seek a sign?"

8:1
Mt 15:32-38
8:2
Ps 111:4, 5
145:9
Mk 1:41
Heb 2:17; 4:15
5:1-3
8:4
Num 11:21, 22
2 Kgs 4:42, 43
8:5
Mk 6:38
8:6
1 Tim 4:4, 5

8:7
Mt 14:19

8:10
Mt 15:39—16:12

8:11
Mt 12:38
16:1-10
Lk 11:16
Jn 6:30
1 Cor 1:22

8:15
Lk 12:1

8:1 This is a different miracle from the feeding of the 5,000 described in chapter 6. At that time, those fed were mostly Jews. This time Jesus was ministering to a Gentile crowd in the Gentile region of the Ten Towns, or Decapolis. Jesus' work and message were beginning to have an impact on large numbers of Gentiles.

8:1-3 Do you ever feel God is so busy with important concerns that he can't possibly be aware of your needs? Just as Jesus was concerned about those people's need for food, he is concerned about our daily needs. At another time Jesus said, "Don't worry at all about having enough food and clothing. Your heavenly Father already knows perfectly well that you need them" (Matthew 6:31, 32). Do you have concerns that you think would not interest God? There is no concern too large for him to handle and no need too small to escape his interest.

8:11 The Pharisees had tried to explain away Jesus' previous miracles by claiming they were done by luck, coincidence, or evil power. So they demanded a sign in the sky—something only God could do. Jesus refused their demand because he knew that even this kind of miracle would not convince them. They had already decided not to believe. Hearts can become so hard that even the most convincing facts and demonstrations will not change them.

8:15ff Yeast in this passage symbolizes evil. As only a small amount of yeast is needed to make a batch of bread rise, so the hardheartedness of the Jewish leaders could permeate and contaminate the entire society and make it rise up against Jesus.

8:15 Mark mentions the "yeast of King Herod and the

¹⁶"What does he mean?" the disciples asked each other. They finally decided that he must be talking about their forgetting to bring bread.

8:17
Mk 6:52
8:18
Ezek 12:2

¹⁷Jesus realized what they were discussing and said, "No, that isn't it at all! Can't you understand? Are your hearts too hard to take it in? ¹⁸'Your eyes are to see with—why don't you look? Why don't you open your ears and listen?' Don't you remember anything at all?

8:19
Mt 14:20
Mk 6:43, 44
Lk 9:17
Jn 6:13
8:20
Mt 15:37
Mk 8:8, 9

¹⁹"What about the 5,000 men I fed with five loaves of bread? How many basketfuls of scraps did you pick up afterwards?"

"Twelve," they said.

²⁰"And when I fed the 4,000 with seven loaves, how much was left?"

"Seven basketfuls," they said.

²¹"And yet you think I'm worried that we have no bread?"

Jesus restores sight to a blind man
(108)

8:23
Mk 7:33
Jn 9:6

²²When they arrived at Bethsaida, some people brought a blind man to him and begged him to touch and heal him. ²³Jesus took the blind man by the hand and led him out of the village, and spat upon his eyes, and laid his hands over them.

"Can you see anything now?" Jesus asked him.

²⁴The man looked around. "Yes!" he said, "I see men! But I can't see them very clearly; they look like tree trunks walking around!"

²⁵Then Jesus placed his hands over the man's eyes again and as the man stared intently, his sight was completely restored, and he saw everything clearly, drinking in the sights around him.

8:26
Mt 8:4

²⁶Jesus sent him home to his family. "Don't even go back to the village first," he said.

Peter says Jesus is the Messiah
(109/Matthew 16:13-20; Luke 9:18-20)

8:27
Mt 16:13-20
Lk 9:18-21

²⁷Jesus and his disciples now left Galilee and went out to the villages of Caesarea Philippi. As they were walking along he asked them, "Who do the people think I am? What are they saying about me?"

8:28
Mt 14:2

²⁸"Some of them think you are John the Baptist," the disciples replied, "and others say you are Elijah or some other ancient prophet come back to life again."

8:21 *And yet you think I'm worried that we have no bread?* literally, "Do you not yet understand?"

Pharisees," while Matthew talks about the "yeast of the Sadducees and Pharisees." Mark's audience, mostly non-Jews, would have known about King Herod, but not necessarily about the Jewish religious sect of the Sadducees. Thus Mark quoted the part of Jesus' statement that his readers would understand. When Mark refers to King Herod he is talking about the Herodians, a group of Jews who supported King Herod. Many Herodians were also Sadducees.

8:17, 18 How could the disciples experience so many of Jesus' miracles and yet be so slow to comprehend his true identity? They had already seen Jesus feed over 5,000 people with five loaves and two fish (6:35-44), yet now they doubted whether he could feed another large group. Sometimes we are also slow to catch on. Although Christ has brought us through trials and temptations in the past, we are slow to believe he will do it in the future. Is your heart too closed to take in all that God can do for you? Don't be like the disciples. Remember what Christ has done, and have faith that he will do it again.

8:25 Why did Jesus touch the man a second time before he could see? This miracle was not too difficult for Jesus, but he chose to do it in stages, possibly to show the disciples that some healing would be gradual rather than instantaneous or to demonstrate that spiritual truth is not always perceived clearly at first. Before Jesus left, however, the man was healed completely.

8:27 Caesarea Philippi was an especially pagan city, known for its worship of Greek gods and its temples devoted to the ancient god Baal. Herod Philip, mentioned in Mark 6:18, changed the city's name from Caesarea to Caesarea Philippi so that it would not be confused with the coastal city of Caesarea (Acts 8:40), the capital of the territory ruled by his brother, Herod Antipas. This pagan city, where many gods were recognized, was a fitting place for Jesus to ask the disciples to recognize his identity as the Son of God.

8:28 For the story of John the Baptist, see Mark 1:1-11 and 6:14-29. For the story of Elijah, see 1 Kings 17-20 and 2 Kings 1, 2.

²⁹ Then he asked, "Who do you think I am?" Peter replied, "You are the Messiah." ³⁰ But Jesus warned them not to tell anyone!

8:29
Jn 6:69; 11:27

Jesus predicts his death the first time
(110/Matthew 16:21–28; Luke 9:21–27)

³¹ Then he began to tell them about the terrible things he would suffer, and that he would be rejected by the elders and the Chief Priests and the other Jewish leaders—and be killed, and that he would rise again three days afterwards. ³² He talked about it quite frankly with them, so Peter took him aside and chided him. "You shouldn't say things like that," he told Jesus.

8:31
Mt 16:21–28; 17:22, 23
Lk 9:22–27

³³ Jesus turned and looked at his disciples and then said to Peter very sternly, "Satan, get behind me! You are looking at this only from a human point of view and not from God's."

8:33
Rom 8:7

³⁴ Then he called his disciples and the crowds to come over and listen. "If any of you wants to be my follower," he told them, "you must put aside your own pleasures and shoulder your cross, and follow me closely. ³⁵ If you insist on saving your life, you will lose it. Only those who throw away their lives for my sake and for the sake of the Good News will ever know what it means to really live.

8:34
Mt 10:38
Lk 14:27
8:35
Lk 17:33
Jn 12:25
Rev 12:11

³⁶ "And how does a man benefit if he gains the whole world and loses his

8:31 *he would suffer,* literally, "the Son of Man would suffer." **8:32** *chided him,* "began to rebuke him."

8:29 Jesus asked the disciples who others thought he was; then he focused on them: "Who do *you* think I am?" It is not enough to know what others say about Jesus: you must know, understand, and accept for yourself that he is the Messiah. You must move from curiosity to commitment, from admiration to adoration.

8:30 Why did Jesus warn his own disciples not to tell anyone the truth about him? Jesus knew they needed more instruction about the work he would accomplish through his death and resurrection. Without more teaching, the disciples would have only half the picture. When they confessed Jesus as the Christ, they still didn't know all that it meant.

8:31 From this point on, Jesus spoke plainly and directly to his disciples about his death and resurrection. He began to prepare them for what was going to happen to him by telling them three times that he would soon die (8:31; 9:31; 10:33, 34).

8:32, 33 In this moment, Peter was not considering God's purposes, but only his natural human desires and feelings. He wanted Christ to be King, but not the suffering servant prophesied in Isaiah 53. He was ready to receive the glory of following the Messiah, but not the persecution. The Christian life is not a paved road to wealth and ease. It often involves hard work, persecution, privation, and deep suffering. Peter saw only part of the picture. Don't repeat his mistake—instead, focus on the good that God can bring out of apparent evil, and the resurrection that follows crucifixion.

8:33 Peter was often the spokesman for all the disciples. In singling him out, Jesus may have been addressing all of them indirectly. Unknowingly, the disciples were trying to prevent Jesus from going to the cross, his real mission on earth. Satan tempted Jesus to do the same thing (Matthew 4). Whereas Satan's motives were evil, the disciples were motivated by love and admiration for Jesus. Nevertheless, the disciples' job was not to guide and protect Jesus, but to follow him. Only after Jesus' death and resurrection would they fully understand why he had to die.

8:34 The Romans, Mark's original audience, knew what shouldering a cross meant. Death on a cross was a form of execution used by Rome for dangerous criminals. A prisoner carried his own cross to the place of execution, signifying submission to Rome's power.

Jesus used carrying a cross to illustrate the ultimate submission required to follow him. He is not against pleasure, nor is he saying that we should seek pain needlessly. He is talking about the heroic effort needed to follow him moment by moment, to do his will even when the work is difficult and the future looks bleak.

8:35 To throw away our lives for the sake of the Good News doesn't mean our lives are useless. Rather, it means that nothing—not even life itself—can compare to what we can gain with Christ. Jesus wants us to *choose* to follow him rather than to lead a life of sin and self-satisfaction. He wants us to stop trying to control our own lives and to let him be in charge. This makes good sense because, as the Creator, only he knows what real life is about. He asks for submission, not self-hatred; he asks us to throw away the self-centeredness that says we know better than God how to run our lives.

8:36, 37 Many people spend their lives seeking pleasure. Jesus said, however, that the world of pleasure centered on possessions, position, or power is ultimately worthless. Whatever we have on earth is only temporary; it cannot be exchanged for our souls. If you work hard at getting what you want, you might eventually have a "pleasurable" life, but in the end you will find it hollow and empty. Are you willing to make the pursuit of God more important than the selfish pursuit of pleasure? Follow Jesus, and you will know what it means to really live in this life and to have life eternal as well.

8:38
Mt 10:33
Lk 12:9
Rom 1:16
2 Thess 1:7
2 Tim 1:8; 2:12
Heb 11:16

soul in the process? [37] For is anything worth more than his soul? [38] And anyone who is ashamed of me and my message in these days of unbelief and sin, I, the Messiah, will be ashamed of him when I return in the glory of my Father, with the holy angels."

9:1
Mt 16:28; 24:30
25:31
Lk 9:27; 22:18

9 Jesus went on to say to his disciples, "Some of you who are standing here right now will live to see the Kingdom of God arrive in great power!"

Jesus is transfigured on the mountain
(111/Matthew 17:1–13; Luke 9:28–36)

9:2
Mt 17:1–13
Lk 9:28–36

[2] Six days later Jesus took Peter, James and John to the top of a mountain. No one else was there.

9:3
Dan 7:9
Mt 28:3

Suddenly his face began to shine with glory, [3] and his clothing became dazzling white, far more glorious than any earthly process could ever make it! [4] Then Elijah and Moses appeared and began talking with Jesus!

[5] "Teacher, this is wonderful!" Peter exclaimed. "We will make three shelters here, one for each of you. . . ."

[6] He said this just to be talking, for he didn't know what else to say and they were all terribly frightened.

9:7
Ex 40:34
2 Pet 1:17, 18
Heb 1:2; 2:3; 12:25

[7] But while he was still speaking these words, a cloud covered them, blotting out the sun, and a voice from the cloud said, *"This* is my beloved Son. Listen to *him."*

[8] Then suddenly they looked around and Moses and Elijah were gone, and only Jesus was with them.

8:38 *the Messiah,* literally, "the Son of Man."

KEY WORDS IN MARK'S GOSPEL	Word	Selected References	Significance
	Follow	1:17; 8:34; 10:21	Christians must be willing to sacrifice everything for Jesus.
	Listen	4:3; 7:14; 9:7	In order to understand Jesus, we must be open to what he says.
	Understand	4:24; 4:33; 7:18	The more we obey Jesus, the more we will understand his message.
	Immediately (Instantly)	1:20; 1:42; 7:35	Mark uses this word to emphasize Jesus' authority and to keep the story fast-paced.
	Kingdom of God	1:15; 4:30–32; 9:47	Jesus' coming signals a new reign of God on earth.

8:38 Jesus constantly turns the world's perspective upside down with talk of saving and losing, throwing away and finding. Here he faces us with a choice. Those so embarrassed by Jesus now that they reject him in this life will see him clearly at the time of judgment, but it will be too late. Those who see him clearly now and accept him will escape the shame of being rejected at his final judgment.

9:1 What did Jesus mean when he said that some of the disciples would see the Kingdom arrive? There are several possibilities. He could have been foretelling his transfiguration, his resurrection and ascension, the coming of the Holy Spirit at Pentecost, or his second coming. The transfiguration is a strong possibility because it follows immediately in the text. In the transfiguration (9:2–8), Peter, James, and John saw Jesus' true identity and power as the Son of God (2 Peter 1:16).

9:2 We don't know why Jesus singled out Peter, James, and John for this special revelation. Perhaps they were the ones most ready to understand and accept this great truth revealed about Jesus. These three disciples were the inner circle of the group of twelve. They were among the

first to hear Jesus' call (1:16–19). They headed the Gospel lists of disciples (3:16). And they were present at certain healings where others were excluded (Luke 8:51).

9:2 Jesus took the disciples to either Mount Hermon or Mount Tabor. A mountain was often associated with closeness to God and readiness to receive his words. God had appeared to both Moses (Exodus 24:12–18) and Elijah (1 Kings 19:8–18) on mountains.

9:3ff The transfiguration revealed Christ's true nature as God's Son. God's voice singled Jesus out from Moses and Elijah as the long-awaited Messiah with full divine authority. Moses represented the law and Elijah, the prophets. With their appearance, Jesus was shown as the fulfillment of both the Old Testament law and the prophetic promises.

Jesus was not a reincarnation of Elijah or Moses. He was not merely one of the prophets. As God's only Son, he far surpasses their authority and power. Many voices try to tell us how to live and how to know God personally. Some of these are helpful; many are not. We must first listen to Jesus, and then evaluate all other authorities in light of his revelation.

9 As they descended the mountainside he told them never to mention what they had seen until after he had risen from the dead. 10 So they kept it to themselves, but often talked about it, and wondered what he meant by "rising from the dead."

11 Now they began asking him about something the Jewish religious leaders often spoke of, that Elijah must return [before the Messiah could come]. 12, 13 Jesus agreed that Elijah must come first and prepare the way—and that he had, in fact, already come! And that he had been terribly mistreated, just as the prophets had predicted. Then Jesus asked them what the prophets could have been talking about when they predicted that the Messiah would suffer and be treated with utter contempt.

9:11
Mal 4:5
Mt 11:14
9:12, 13
Gen 3:15
Ps 22:6, 7
Isa 50:6; 53:2, 3
Dan 9:26
Mt 11:13, 14
Lk 1:17; 23:11
Jn 3:14

Jesus heals a demon-possessed boy
(112/Matthew 17:14–21; Luke 9:37–43)

14 At the bottom of the mountain they found a great crowd surrounding the other nine disciples, as some Jewish leaders argued with them. 15 The crowd watched Jesus in awe as he came toward them, and then ran to greet him. 16 "What's all the argument about?" he asked.

9:14
Mt 17:14–21
Lk 9:37–43

17 One of the men in the crowd spoke up and said, "Teacher, I brought my son for you to heal—he can't talk because he is possessed by a demon. 18 And whenever the demon is in control of him it dashes him to the ground and makes him foam at the mouth and grind his teeth and become rigid. So I begged your disciples to cast out the demon, but they couldn't do it."

19 Jesus said [to his disciples], "Oh, what tiny faith you have; how much longer must I be with you until you believe? How much longer must I be patient with you? Bring the boy to me."

9:19
Jn 4:48

20 So they brought the boy, but when he saw Jesus the demon convulsed the child horribly, and he fell to the ground writhing and foaming at the mouth. 21 "How long has he been this way?" Jesus asked the father.

9:20
Mk 1:26

And he replied, "Since he was very small, 22 and the demon often makes him fall into the fire or into water to kill him. Oh, have mercy on us and do something if you can."

23 "If I can?" Jesus asked. *"Anything* is possible if you have faith."

9:23
Mk 11:22–24
Lk 17:6
Jn 11:40
Acts 14:9

9:9 *after he had risen,* literally, "after the Son of Man had risen." **9:11** *before the Messiah could come,* implied. **9:12, 13** *the Messiah,* literally, "the Son of Man." **9:18** *and become rigid,* or, "is growing weaker day by day." **9:19** *to his disciples,* implied. *Oh, what tiny faith you have,* literally, "O unbelieving generation."

9:9, 10 Jesus instructed Peter, James, and John not to speak about what they had seen because they would not fully understand what they saw until Jesus had risen from the dead. Then they would realize that only through death could he rise again, showing his power over death and his authority to be King of all. The disciples could not be powerful witnesses for God until they had grasped this truth completely.

It was natural for the disciples to be confused about Jesus' death and resurrection because they could not see into the future. We, on the other hand, have God's entire revealed Word, the Bible, to give us the full meaning of Jesus' death and resurrection. We have no excuse for our unbelief.

9:11-13 When Jesus said Elijah had indeed come, he was speaking of John the Baptist (Matthew 17:11-13).

9:12, 13 It was difficult for the disciples to understand that their Messiah would have to suffer. The Jews who studied the Old Testament prophecies expected the Messiah to be a great king like David, who would overthrow the enemy, Rome. Their vision was limited to their own time and experience.

They could not grasp that the values of God's eternal kingdom were different from the values of the world. They wanted relief from their present problems, but deliverance from sin is far more important than deliverance from physical suffering or political oppression. Our understanding of and appreciation for Jesus must go beyond what he can do for us here and now.

9:18 Why couldn't the disciples cast out the demon? In Mark 6:12 we read that they cast out demons while on their mission to the villages. Perhaps they had special authority only for that trip; or perhaps their faith had lapsed. Mark tells this story to show that the battle with Satan is a difficult, ongoing struggle. Victory over sin and temptation comes through faith in Jesus Christ, not through our own effort.

9:23 These words of Jesus do not mean we can automatically obtain anything we want if we just think positively. Jesus meant that anything is *possible* with faith because nothing is too difficult for God. This is not a teaching on how to pray as much as a statement about God's power to overcome obstacles to his work. We cannot have everything we pray for as if by magic; but with faith, we can have everything we need to serve him.

9:24
Eph 2:8
9:25
Acts 10:38

24 The father instantly replied, "I *do* have faith; oh, help me to have *more!*"
25 When Jesus saw the crowd was growing he rebuked the demon.

"O demon of deafness and dumbness," he said, "I command you to come out of this child and enter him no more!"

26 Then the demon screamed terribly and convulsed the boy again and left him; and the boy lay there limp and motionless, to all appearance dead. A murmur ran through the crowd—"He is dead." 27 But Jesus took him by the hand and helped him to his feet and he stood up and was all right! 28 Afterwards, when Jesus was alone in the house with his disciples, they asked him, "Why couldn't we cast that demon out?"

29 Jesus replied, "Cases like this require prayer."

Jesus predicts his death the second time
(113/Matthew 17:22, 23; Luke 9:44, 45)

9:30
Mt 17:22, 23
Lk 9:43–45
9:31
Mt 16:21
Mk 8:31
Lk 9:22

30, 31 Leaving that region they traveled through Galilee where he tried to avoid all publicity in order to spend more time with his disciples, teaching them. He would say to them, "I, the Messiah, am going to be betrayed and killed and three days later I will return to life again."

32 But they didn't understand and were afraid to ask him what he meant.

The disciples argue about who would be the greatest
(115/Matthew 18:1–6; Luke 9:46–48)

9:33
Mt 18:1–11
Lk 9:46–50

33 And so they arrived at Capernaum. When they were settled in the house where they were to stay he asked them, "What were you discussing out on the road?"

9:34
Prov 13:10
Lk 22:24, 26

34 But they were ashamed to answer, for they had been arguing about which of them was the greatest!

9:35
Mt 20:26, 27; 23:11
Mk 10:43, 44

35 He sat down and called them around him and said, "Anyone wanting to be the greatest must be the least—the servant of all!"

36 Then he placed a little child among them; and taking the child in his arms

9:29 *Cases like this require prayer.* "And fasting" is added in some manuscripts, but not the most ancient.

9:24 Faith is not something tangible to be taken like medicine. It is an attitude of trusting and believing (Hebrews 11:1, 6). But even our ability to believe is a gift from God (Ephesians 2:8, 9). No matter how much faith we have, we never reach the point of being self-sufficient. Faith is not stored away like money in the bank. Growing in faith is a constant process of daily renewing our trust in Jesus.

9:29 Jesus was telling the disciples that they would face difficult situations that could be resolved only through prayer. Prayer is the key that unlocks faith in our lives. Effective prayer needs both an attitude—complete dependence—and an action—asking. Prayer demonstrates our reliance on God as we humbly invite God to fill us with faith and power. There is no substitute for prayer, especially in circumstances that seem unconquerable.

9:30, 31 At times Jesus limited his public ministry in order to train his disciples in depth. He knew the importance of equipping them to carry on when he returned to heaven. It takes time to learn. Deep spiritual growth isn't instant, regardless of the quality of experience or teaching. If even the disciples needed to lay aside their work periodically in order to learn from the Master, how much more do we need to alternate working and learning.

9:30, 31 Leaving Caesarea Philippi, Jesus began his last tour through the region of Galilee.

9:32 Why were the disciples afraid to ask Jesus about his prediction of his death? Perhaps it was because the last time they reacted to Jesus' words they were scolded (8:32, 33). In their minds, Jesus seemed morbidly preoccupied with death. Actually it was the disciples who were wrongly preoccupied—constantly thinking about the kingdom they hoped Jesus would bring and their positions in it. They were worried about what would happen to them if Jesus died, and consequently they preferred not to talk about his predictions.

9:34 The disciples had been caught up in their constant struggle for personal success, and they were embarrassed to answer Jesus' question. It is always painful to compare our motives with Christ's. It is not wrong for believers to be industrious or ambitious, but inappropriate ambition is sin. Pride or insecurity can cause us to value position and prestige more than service. In God's kingdom, such motives are destructive. Our ambition should be for Christ's kingdom, not for our own advancement.

9:36, 42 Luke 9:48 states, "Your care for others is the measure of greatness." In Jesus' eyes, whoever welcomes a child welcomes Jesus; giving a cup of cold water to one in need is the same as giving an offering to God. By contrast, harming others or even failing to care for them is a sin. It is possible for thoughtless, selfish people to gain a measure of greatness in the world's eyes, but enduring greatness is measured only by God's

he said to them, [37] "Anyone who welcomes a little child like this in my name is welcoming me, and anyone who welcomes me is welcoming my Father who sent me!"

9:37
Mt 10:40
Mk 10:16
Jn 13:20

The disciples forbid another to use Jesus' name
(116/Luke 9:49, 50)

[38] One of his disciples, John, told him one day, "Teacher, we saw a man using your name to cast out demons; but we told him not to, for he isn't one of our group."

9:38
Num 11:26–29

[39] "Don't forbid him!" Jesus said. "For no one doing miracles in my name will quickly turn against me. [40] Anyone who isn't against us is for us. [41] If anyone so much as gives you a cup of water because you are Christ's—I say this solemnly—he won't lose his reward. [42] But if someone causes one of these little ones who believe in me to lose faith—it would be better for that man if a huge millstone were tied around his neck and he were thrown into the sea.

9:39
1 Cor 12:3
9:40
Mt 12:30
9:41
Mt 10:42
9:42
Lk 17:1–3
9:43
Deut 13:6–10
Mt 5:29, 30
Rom 8:12, 13
Col 3:5
Heb 12:1

Jesus warns against temptation
(117/Matthew 18:7–9)

[43, 44] "If your hand does wrong, cut it off. Better live forever with one hand than be thrown into the unquenchable fires of hell with two! [45, 46] If your foot carries you toward evil, cut it off! Better be lame and live forever than have two feet that carry you to hell.

9:48
Isa 66:24
2 Thess 1:9
9:49
Lev 2:13
Ezek 43:24

[47] "And if your eye is sinful, gouge it out. Better enter the Kingdom of God half blind than have two eyes and see the fires of hell, [48] where the worm never dies, and the fire never goes out— [49] where all are salted with fire.

9:50
Mt 5:13
Lk 14:34
Rom 12:18
Eph 4:29
Col 4:6
1 Thess 5:13
Heb 12:14

[50] "Good salt is worthless if it loses its saltiness; it can't season anything. So don't lose your flavor! Live in peace with each other."

9:39 *will quickly turn against me,* literally, "will be able to speak evil of me." **9:43, 44** Vss 44, 46 (which are identical with vs 48) are omitted in some of the ancient manuscripts. **9:49** *where all are salted with fire,* literally, "For everyone shall be salted with fire."

---

standards. What do you use as your measure of greatness—personal achievement or unselfish service?

9:36, 37 Jesus taught the disciples to welcome the children. This was a new approach in a society where children were usually treated as second-class citizens. It is important not only to treat children well, but also to teach them about Jesus. Sunday School should never be regarded as less important than adult Bible study.

9:38 More concerned about their own group's position than in helping free those troubled by demons, the disciples were jealous of a man who healed in Jesus' name. We do the same today when we refuse to participate in worthy causes because (1) they are not affiliated with our denomination, (2) they do not involve the kind of people with whom we feel most comfortable, (3) they don't do things the way we are used to, (4) our efforts don't receive enough recognition. Correct theology is important, but it should never be an excuse to avoid helping those in need.

9:40 Jesus was not saying that being indifferent or neutral toward him is as good as being committed. As he explained in Matthew 12:30, "Anyone who isn't helping me is harming me." Jesus taught that many different people follow him and do work in his name, and they should all get along. Those who share a common faith in Christ should be able to cooperate. People don't have to be just like us to be following Jesus with us.

9:42 This caution against harming little ones in the faith applies both to what we do individually as teachers and examples and to what we allow in our Christian

fellowship. Our thoughts and actions must be motivated by love (1 Corinthians 13) and we must be careful about judging others (Matthew 7:1–5; Romans 14:1—15:4). However, we also have a responsibility to confront flagrant sin within the church (1 Corinthians 5:12, 13).

9:43ff Jesus used startling language to stress the importance of cutting sin out of our lives. Painful discipline is required of his true followers. Giving up a relationship, job, or habit that is against God's will may seem just as painful as cutting off a hand. Our high goal, however, is worth any sacrifice; Christ is worth any possible loss. Nothing should stand in the way of faith. We must be ruthless in removing sins from our lives now in order to avoid being stuck with them for eternity. Make your choices from an eternal perspective.

9:48, 49 With these strange words, Jesus pictured the serious and eternal consequences of sin. To the Jews, worms and fire represented both internal and external pain. What could be worse?

9:50 Jesus used salt to illustrate three qualities which should be found in the lives of his people: (1) *We should remember God's faithfulness,* just as salt was used with a sacrifice to recall God's covenant with his people (Leviticus 2:13). (2) *We should be effective in Christian living,* just as salt is effective in giving flavor to food (see Matthew 5:13). When we lose this desire to "salt" the earth with the love and message of God, we become useless to him. (3) *We should live morally* so that we can counteract the decay in society, just as salt preserves food from decay.

Jesus teaches about marriage and divorce
(173/Matthew 19:1–12)

10 Then he left Capernaum and went southward to the Judean borders and into the area east of the Jordan River. And as always there were the crowds; and as usual he taught them.

10:2
Mt 19:3–12

² Some Pharisees came and asked him, "Do you permit divorce?" Of course they were trying to trap him.

³ "What did Moses say about divorce?" Jesus asked them.

10:4
Deut 24:1–3
Mt 5:31

⁴ "He said it was all right," they replied. "He said that all a man has to do is write his wife a letter of dismissal."

10:6
Gen 1:27; 2:24

⁵ "And why did he say that?" Jesus asked. "I'll tell you why—it was a concession to your hardhearted wickedness. ⁶, ⁷ But it certainly isn't God's way. For from the very first he made man and woman to be joined together permanently in marriage; therefore a man is to leave his father and mother,

10:8
1 Cor 6:16
Eph 5:31

⁸ and he and his wife are united so that they are no longer two, but one. ⁹ And no man may separate what God has joined together."

¹⁰ Later, when he was alone with his disciples in the house, they brought up the subject again.

10:11
Mt 5:32
Lk 16:18
Rom 7:2, 3

¹¹ He told them, "When a man divorces his wife to marry someone else, he commits adultery against her. ¹² And if a wife divorces her husband and remarries, she, too, commits adultery."

Jesus blesses little children
(174/Matthew 19:13–15; Luke 18:15–17)

10:13
Mt 19:13–15
Lk 18:15–17

¹³ Once when some mothers were bringing their children to Jesus to bless them, the disciples shooed them away, telling them not to bother him.

10:1 *Then he left Capernaum,* literally, "And rising up, he went from there." Mentioned here so quietly, this was his final farewell to Galilee. He never returned until after his death and resurrection. **10:13** *mothers,* implied.

FINAL TRIP TO JUDEA
Jesus quietly left Capernaum, heading toward the borders of Judea before crossing the Jordan River. He preached there before going to Jericho. This trip from Galilee was his last; he would not return before his death.

thinking about what God intended for marriage, but had settled for marriages of convenience. In addition, they were quoting Moses unfairly and out of context. Jesus showed these legal experts how superficial their knowledge really was.

10:5–9 God allowed divorce as a concession to people's sinfulness. Divorce was not approved, but it was instituted to protect the injured party in the midst of a bad situation. Unfortunately, the Pharisees used Deuteronomy 24:1 as an excuse for divorce. Jesus explained that this was not God's intent; instead, God wants married people to consider their marriage permanent. Don't enter marriage with the option of getting out, but be committed to permanence. You'll stand a much better chance of making your marriage work. Don't be hard-hearted like these Pharisees, but be hardheaded in your determination, with God's help, to stay together.

10:6, 7 Women were often treated as property. Marriage and divorce were regarded as transactions similar to buying and selling land. But Jesus condemned this practice, clarifying God's original intention—that marriage bring oneness (Genesis 2:24). Jesus held up God's ideal for marriage and told his followers to live by it.

10:13–16 Jesus was often criticized for spending too much time with the wrong people—children, sinners (Matthew 9:11), tax collectors (Luke 15:1, 2; 19:7). Some, including the disciples, thought Jesus should be spending more time with important leaders and the devout, because this was the way to improve his position and avoid criticism. But Jesus didn't need to improve his position. He was God, and he wanted to speak to those who needed him most.

10:2 The Pharisees were trying to trap Jesus with their question. If Jesus said he supported divorce, he would be upholding the Pharisees' procedures; and they doubted that he would do that. If he spoke against divorce, however, the crowds would dislike his position. More important, he might incur the wrath of King Herod, who had already killed John the Baptist for speaking out against divorce and adultery (6:17–28). This is what the Pharisees wanted.

The Pharisees saw divorce as a legal issue rather than a spiritual one. Jesus used this test as an opportunity to review God's intended purpose for marriage and to expose the Pharisees' selfish motives. They were not

¹⁴ But when Jesus saw what was happening he was very much displeased with his disciples and said to them, "Let the children come to me, for the Kingdom of God belongs to such as they. Don't send them away! ¹⁵ I tell you as seriously as I know how that anyone who refuses to come to God as a little child will never be allowed into his Kingdom."

10:15
Mt 18:3
1 Cor 14:20
1 Pet 2:2

¹⁶ Then he took the children into his arms and placed his hands on their heads and he blessed them.

10:16
Isa 40:11

Jesus speaks to the rich young man
(175/Matthew 19:16–30; Luke 18:18–30)

¹⁷ As he was starting out on a trip, a man came running to him and knelt down and asked, "Good Teacher, what must I do to get to heaven?"

10:17
Mt 19:16–30
Lk 18:18–30

¹⁸ "Why do you call me good?" Jesus asked. "Only God is truly good! ¹⁹ But as for your question—you know the commandments: don't kill, don't commit adultery, don't steal, don't lie, don't cheat, respect your father and mother."

10:19
Ex 20:12–17
Deut 5:16–20
Rom 13:9

²⁰ "Teacher," the man replied, "I've never once broken a single one of those laws."

10:20
Jas 2:10

²¹ Jesus felt genuine love for this man as he looked at him. "You lack only one thing," he told him; "go and sell all you have and give the money to the poor—and you shall have treasure in heaven—and come, follow me."

10:21
Mt 6:19, 20
Lk 12:33
Acts 2:44, 45
1 Tim 6:17–19

²² Then the man's face fell, and he went sadly away, for he was very rich.

²³ Jesus watched him go, then turned around and said to his disciples, "It's almost impossible for the rich to get into the Kingdom of God!"

²⁴ This amazed them. So Jesus said it again: "Dear children, how hard it is for those who trust in riches to enter the Kingdom of God. ²⁵ It is easier for a camel to go through the eye of a needle than for a rich man to enter the Kingdom of God."

10:24
Ps 52:7

10:20 *never once*, literally, "from my youth." **10:24** *for those who trust in riches.* Some of the ancient manuscripts do not contain the words, "for those who trust in riches."

10:14 Adults are not as trusting as little children. All children need in order to feel secure is a loving look and gentle touch from someone who cares. Complete intellectual understanding is not one of their requirements. They believe us if they trust us. Jesus said that all must believe in him with this kind of childlike faith. We should not have to understand all the mysteries of the universe; it should be enough to know that God loves us and provides forgiveness for our sin. This doesn't mean we should be childish or immature, but we should trust God with a child's simplicity and purity.

10:17-23 This young man wanted to be sure he would get eternal life, so he asked what he could *do*. He said he'd never once broken any of the laws Jesus mentioned (verse 19), and perhaps he had kept the Pharisees' loophole-filled version of them. But Jesus lovingly broke through his pride with a challenge that brought out his true motives: "Sell all you have and give to the poor." Here was the barrier that could keep this young man out of the Kingdom: his love of money. Money represented his pride of accomplishment and self-effort. Ironically, his attitude made him unable to keep the first commandment, to let nothing be more important than God (Exodus 20:3). He could not meet the one requirement Jesus gave—to turn his whole heart and life over to God. The man came to Jesus wondering what he could do; he left seeing what he was unable to do. What barriers are keeping you from turning your life over to Christ?

10:18 When Jesus asked this question, he was saying, "Do you really know to whom you are talking?" Because only God is truly good, the man was calling Jesus God. This was true, of course, but he may not have realized it.

10:21 What does your money mean to you? Although Jesus wanted this man to sell everything and give his money to the poor, this does not mean that all believers should sell all their possessions. Most of his followers did not sell everything, although they used their possessions to bless others. Instead, this story shows us that we must not let anything keep us from following Jesus. We should remove all barriers to serving him fully. If Jesus asked you to, could you give up your house? your car? your way of eating? Could you move to a crowded apartment in a poor neighborhood, ride the city buses, and never know where your next meal was coming from, if that was how Jesus wanted you to serve him? Your reaction may show your attitude toward money—whether it is your servant or your master.

10:21 Jesus showed genuine love for this man, even though he knew he might not follow him. Genuine love is able to give tough advice; it doesn't hedge around the truth. Christ loved us enough to die for us, but he still gives tough advice. If his love were superficial, he would give us only approval; but because his love is complete, he gives us life-changing challenges.

10:23 Jesus said it was very difficult for the rich to get into the kingdom of God because the rich have most of their basic physical needs met and can become self-reliant. When they feel empty, they can buy something new to dull the pain that was meant to drive them toward God. Their abundance becomes their deficiency. The person who has everything on earth can still lack what is most important—eternal life.

26 The disciples were incredulous! "Then who in the world can be saved, if not a rich man?" they asked.

27 Jesus looked at them intently, then said, "Without God, it is utterly impossible. But with God everything is possible."

28 Then Peter began to mention all that he and the other disciples had left behind. "We've given up everything to follow you," he said.

29 And Jesus replied, "Let me assure you that no one has ever given up anything—home, brothers, sisters, mother, father, children, or property—for love of me and to tell others the Good News, 30 who won't be given back, a hundred times over, homes, brothers, sisters, mothers, children, and land— with persecutions!

"All these will be his here on earth, and in the world to come he shall have eternal life. 31 But many people who seem to be important now will be the least important then; and many who are considered least here shall be greatest there."

Jesus predicts his death the third time
(177/Matthew 20:17-19; Luke 18:31-34)

32 Now they were on the way to Jerusalem, and Jesus was walking along ahead; and as the disciples were following they were filled with terror and dread.

Taking them aside, Jesus once more began describing all that was going to happen to him when they arrived at Jerusalem.

33 "When we get there," he told them, "I, the Messiah, will be arrested and taken before the chief priests and the Jewish leaders, who will sentence me to die and hand me over to the Romans to be killed. 34 They will mock me and spit on me and flog me with their whips and kill me; but after three days I will come back to life again."

Jesus teaches about serving others
(178/Matthew 20:20-28)

35 Then James and John, the sons of Zebedee, came over and spoke to him in a low voice. "Master," they said, "we want you to do us a favor."
36 "What is it?" he asked.

10:33 *the Messiah,* literally, "the Son of Man." 10:35 *spoke to him in a low voice,* literally, "came up to him."

10:27 Jer 32:17 / Heb 7:25
10:28 Mk 1:18
10:30 Acts 14:22 / 1 Thess 3:3 / 2 Tim 3:12
10:31 Mt 20:16 / Lk 13:30
10:32 Mt 20:17-19 / Lk 18:31-34
10:33 Mt 16:21; 26:67 / 27:30 / Mk 8:31; 9:31; 14:65 / Lk 9:22 / 1 Cor 15:3, 4
10:35 Mt 20:20-28

10:26 The disciples were incredulous. Was not wealth a blessing from God, a reward for being good? This misconception is still common today. Although many believers enjoy material prosperity, many others live in hardship. Wealth is not a sign of faith or of partiality on God's part.

10:29, 30 Jesus assured the disciples that anyone who gives up something valuable for his sake will be repaid a hundred times over in this life, although not necessarily in the same form. For example, someone may be rejected by his family for accepting Christ, but he will gain the larger family of believers. Along with these rewards, however, we receive persecution because the world hates God. Jesus emphasized persecution to make sure we do not selfishly follow him only for the rewards.

10:31 Jesus explained that in the world to come, the values of this world will be reversed. Those who seek status and importance here will have none in heaven. Those who are humble here will be great in heaven. The corrupt condition of our society encourages this confusion in values. We are bombarded by messages that tell us how to be important and feel good, and Jesus' teaching on service to others seems alien. But those who serve others are most qualified to be great in heaven.

10:32 The disciples were afraid of what they thought awaited them in Jerusalem because Jesus had just spoken to them about facing persecution.

10:33 Jesus' death and resurrection should have come as no surprise to the disciples. Here he clearly explained to them what would happen to him. Unfortunately, they didn't really hear what he was saying. Jesus said he was the Messiah, but they thought the Messiah would be a conquering king. He spoke to them of resurrection, but they wondered how a person could come back to life after being dead. Because Jesus often spoke in parables, the disciples may have thought his words on death and resurrection were another parable they didn't understand. The Gospels include Jesus' predictions of his death and resurrection to show that they were God's plan from the beginning, not an accident.

10:35 Mark records that John and James went to Jesus with their request; in Matthew, their mother also made the request. There is no contradiction in the accounts— mother and sons were in agreement in making the request for honored places in Christ's Kingdom.

37 "We want to sit on the thrones next to yours in your kingdom," they said, "one at your right and the other at your left!"

38 But Jesus answered, "You don't know what you are asking! Are you able to drink from the bitter cup of sorrow I must drink from? Or to be baptized with the baptism of suffering I must be baptized with?"

10:38
Lk 12:50

39 "Oh, yes," they said, "we are!"

And Jesus said, "You shall indeed drink from my cup and be baptized with my baptism, 40 but I do not have the right to place you on thrones next to mine. Those appointments have already been made."

10:39
Acts 12:2
Rev 1:9
10:40
Jas 4:3

41 When the other disciples discovered what James and John had asked, they were very indignant. 42 So Jesus called them to him and said, "As you know, the kings and great men of the earth lord it over the people; 43 but among you it is different. Whoever wants to be great among you must be your servant. 44 And whoever wants to be greatest of all must be the slave of all. 45 For even I, the Messiah, am not here to be served, but to help others, and to give my life as a ransom for many."

10:42
Lk 22:25, 26
10:43
Mk 9:35
Lk 9:48
10:45
Jn 13:14
Phil 2:7
1 Tim 2:5, 6
Tit 2:14

Jesus heals a blind beggar
(179/Matthew 20:29–34; Luke 18:35–43)

46 And so they reached Jericho. Later, as they left town, a great crowd was following. Now it happened that a blind beggar named Bartimaeus (the son of Timaeus) was sitting beside the road as Jesus was going by.

10:46
Mt 20:29–34
Lk 18:35–43

47 When Bartimaeus heard that Jesus from Nazareth was near, he began to shout out, "Jesus, Son of David, have mercy on me!"

10:47
Isa 11:1
Jer 23:5, 6
Rom 1:3
Rev 22:16

48 "Shut up!" some of the people yelled at him.

But he only shouted the louder, again and again, "O Son of David, have mercy on me!"

49 When Jesus heard him he stopped there in the road and said, "Tell him to come here."

So they called the blind man. "You lucky fellow," they said, "come on, he's calling you!" 50 Bartimaeus yanked off his old coat and flung it aside, jumped up and came to Jesus.

10:45 *the Messiah,* literally, "the Son of Man." **10:49** *You lucky fellow,* literally, "be of good cheer."

10:37 The disciples, like most Jews of that day, had the wrong idea of the Messiah's kingdom as predicted by the Old Testament prophets. They thought Jesus would establish an earthly kingdom that would free Israel from Rome's oppression, and James and John wanted honored places in it. But Jesus' kingdom is not of this world; it is not centered in palaces and thrones, but in the hearts and lives of his followers. The disciples did not understand this until after Jesus' resurrection.

10:38 James and John said they were willing to face any trial for Christ. Both did suffer: James died as a martyr (Acts 12:2) and John was forced to live in exile (Revelation 1:9). It is easy to say we'll suffer anything for Christ, and yet most of us complain every day when even little irritations come. If we say we are willing to suffer on a large scale for Christ, we must also be willing to suffer in little ways.

10:38 Jesus didn't ridicule James and John for asking, but he denied their request. We can feel free to ask God for anything, but we may be denied. God wants to give us what is best for us, not merely what we want. Some requests are denied for our own good.

10:42–44 James and John wanted the highest positions in Jesus' kingdom. But Jesus told them that true greatness comes in serving others. Peter, one of the disciples who heard this message, expands this thought in

1 Peter 5:1–4. Most businesses, organizations, and institutions in our world measure greatness by high personal achievement. In Christ's kingdom, however, service is the way to get ahead. The desire to be on top won't be a help but a hindrance.

10:45 A ransom was the price paid to release a slave. Jesus paid a ransom for us, since we could not pay it ourselves. His death released all of us from our slavery to sin. That is why Christ died. The disciples thought Jesus' life and power would save them from Rome; Jesus said his *death* would save them from sin, an even greater slavery than Rome's. More about the ransom Jesus paid for us is found in 1 Peter 1:18, 19.

10:46 Jericho was a popular resort city rebuilt by Herod the Great in the Judean desert, not far from the Jordan River crossing. Jesus was on his way to Jerusalem (verse 32) and, after crossing over from Perea, would naturally enter Jericho.

10:46 Beggars were a common sight in most towns. Since most occupations of that day required physical labor, anyone with a crippling disease or handicap was at a severe disadvantage and was usually forced to beg, even though God's laws commanded care for such needy people (Leviticus 25:35–38). Blindness was considered a curse from God for sin; but Jesus refuted this idea when he reached out to heal those who were blind.

10:52
Isa 35:5
Mt 9:22

51 "What do you want me to do for you?" Jesus asked.

"O Teacher," the blind man said, "I want to see!"

52 And Jesus said to him, "All right, it's done. Your faith has healed you." And instantly the blind man could see, and followed Jesus down the road!

3. Jesus' ministry in Jerusalem

Jesus rides into Jerusalem on a donkey
(183/Matthew 21:1–11; Luke 19:28–44; John 12:12–19)

11:1
Mt 21:1–9
Lk 19:29–40
Jn 12:12–19
Acts 1:12

11 As they neared Bethphage and Bethany on the outskirts of Jerusalem and came to the Mount of Olives, Jesus sent two of his disciples on ahead.

2 "Go into that village over there," he told them, "and just as you enter you will see a colt tied up that has never been ridden. Untie him and bring him here. 3 And if anyone asks you what you are doing, just say, 'Our Master needs him and will return him soon.' "

10:52 *All right, it's done,* literally. "Go your way."

KEY CHARACTER- ISTICS OF CHRIST IN THE GOSPELS

Characteristic	References
Jesus is the Son of God	Matthew 16:15, 16; Mark 1:1 Luke 22:70, 71; John 8:24
Jesus is God who became human	John 1:1, 2, 14; 20:28
Jesus is the Christ, the Messiah	Matthew 26:63, 64; Mark 14:61, 62 Luke 9:20; John 4:25, 26
Jesus came to help sinners	Luke 5:32; Matthew 9:13
Jesus has power to forgive sins	Mark 2:9–12; Luke 24:47
Jesus has authority over death	Mark 5:22–24, 35–42 John 11:1–44; Luke 24:5, 6 Matthew 28:5, 6
Jesus has power to give eternal life	John 10:28; 17:2
Jesus healed the sick	Matthew 8:5–13; Mark 1:32–34 Luke 5:12–15; John 9:1–7
Jesus taught with authority	Mark 1:21, 22; Matthew 7:29
Jesus was compassionate	Mark 1:41; Mark 8:3; Matthew 9:36
Jesus experienced sorrow	Matthew 26:38; John 11:35
Jesus never disobeyed God	Matthew 3:15; John 8:46

JESUS NEARS JERUSALEM
Leaving Jericho, Jesus headed toward acclaim, then crucifixion, in Jerusalem. During his last week, he stayed outside the city in Bethany, a village on the Mount of Olives, entering Jerusalem to teach, eat the Passover, and finally be crucified.

11:1, 2 This was Sunday of the week Jesus would be crucified, and the great Passover festival was about to begin. Jews came to Jerusalem from all over the Roman world during this week-long celebration to remember the great exodus from Egypt (see Exodus 13). Many in the crowds had heard of or seen Jesus and were hoping he would come to the Temple (John 11:55–57).

Jesus did come, not as a king, but on a donkey's colt that had never been ridden. Kings often rode to war on horses or in wheeled vehicles, but Zechariah 9:9 had predicted that the Messiah would come in peace riding on a lowly donkey. Jesus knew that those who heard him teach at the Temple would return to their homes throughout the world and announce the coming of the Messiah.

^{4, 5} Off went the two men and found the colt standing in the street, tied outside a house. As they were untying it, some who were standing there demanded, "What are you doing, untying that colt?"

⁶ So they said what Jesus had told them to, and then the men agreed.

⁷ So the colt was brought to Jesus and the disciples threw their cloaks across its back for him to ride on. ⁸ Then many in the crowd spread out their coats along the road before him, while others threw down leafy branches from the fields.

11:7
Zech 9:9

⁹ He was in the center of the procession with crowds ahead and behind, and all of them shouting, "Hail to the King!" "Praise God for him who comes in the name of the Lord!" . . . ¹⁰ "Praise God for the return of our father David's kingdom. . . ." "Hail to the King of the universe!"

11:9
Ps 118:25, 26

¹¹ And so he entered Jerusalem and went into the Temple. He looked around carefully at everything and then left—for now it was late in the afternoon—and went out to Bethany with the twelve disciples.

11:11
Mt 21:10, 17

Jesus clears the Temple again
(184/Matthew 21:12–17; Luke 19:45–48)

¹² The next morning as they left Bethany, he felt hungry. ¹³ A little way off he noticed a fig tree in full leaf, so he went over to see if he could find any figs on it. But no, there were only leaves, for it was too early in the season for fruit.

11:12-14
Mt 21:18, 19

¹⁴ Then Jesus said to the tree, "You shall never bear fruit again!" And the disciples heard him say it.

¹⁵ When they arrived back to Jerusalem he went to the Temple and began to drive out the merchants and their customers, and knocked over the tables of

11:15
Mt 21:12-17
Lk 19:45–48
Jn 2:13-17

11:9, 10 The people exclaimed "Hail to the king!" They were fulfilling the prophecy in Zechariah 9:9. (See also Psalm 24:7–10; 118:26.) They spoke of the return of David's kingdom because of God's words to David in 2 Samuel 7:12-14. The crowd correctly saw Jesus as the fulfillment of these prophecies, but they did not understand where Jesus' kingship would lead him. This same crowd cried out, "Crucify him!" when Jesus stood on trial only a few days later.

11:11-24 There are two parts to this unusual incident: the cursing of the fig tree and the cleansing of the Temple. The cursing of the fig tree was an acted-out parable related to the cleansing of the Temple. The Temple was supposed to be a place of worship, but true worship had disappeared. The fig tree showed promise of fruit, but it produced none. Jesus was showing his anger at religious life without substance. If you "go through the motions" of faith without putting it to work in your life, you are like the fig tree that withered and died. Genuine faith has great potential; ask God to help you bear fruit for his kingdom.

11:13-25 Fig trees, an inexpensive and popular source of food in Israel, require three years from the time they are planted until they can bear fruit. Each tree yields a great amount of fruit, which is harvested twice a year in late spring and in early autumn. This incident occurred early in the spring fig season when the leaves were beginning to bud. The figs normally grow as the leaves fill out, but this tree, though full of leaves, had no figs; thus, it would not have given fruit that year. The tree looked promising, but offered no fruit. Jesus' harsh words meant that the nation of Israel was like the fig tree. It was supposed to be fruitful, but was spiritually barren.

11:14, 15 Jesus became angry, but he did not sin in his anger. There is a place for righteous indignation. Christians should be upset about sin and injustice and should take a stand against them. Unfortunately, believers

are often passive about these important issues and get angry instead over personal insults and petty irritations. Make sure your anger is directed toward the right issues.

11:15-17 Moneychangers and merchants did big business during Passover. Those who came from foreign countries had to have their money changed into Jewish

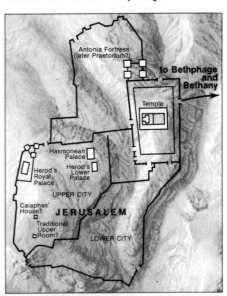

CLEANSING THE TEMPLE On Monday morning of his last week, Jesus left Bethany with his disciples, entered Jerusalem, and cleansed the Temple of moneychangers and merchants.

the moneychangers and the stalls of those selling doves, [16] and stopped everyone from bringing in loads of merchandise.

[17] He told them, "It is written in the Scriptures, 'My Temple is to be a place of prayer for all nations,' but you have turned it into a den of robbers."

[18] When the chief priests and other Jewish leaders heard what he had done they began planning how best to get rid of him. Their problem was their fear of riots because the people were so enthusiastic about Jesus' teaching.

[19] That evening as usual they left the city.

Jesus says the disciples can pray for anything
(188/Matthew 21:18–22)

[20] Next morning, as the disciples passed the fig tree he had cursed, they saw that it was withered from the roots! [21] Then Peter remembered what Jesus had said to the tree on the previous day, and exclaimed, "Look, Teacher! The fig tree you cursed has withered!"

[22, 23] In reply Jesus said to the disciples, "If you only have faith in God— this is the absolute truth—you can say to this Mount of Olives, 'Rise up and fall into the Mediterranean,' and your command will be obeyed. All that's required is that you really believe and have no doubt! [24] Listen to me! You can pray for *anything*, and *if you believe, you have it;* it's yours! [25] But when you are praying, first forgive anyone you are holding a grudge against, so that your Father in heaven will forgive you your sins too."

Religious leaders challenge Jesus' authority
(189/Matthew 21:23–27; Luke 20:1–8)

[26, 27, 28] By this time they had arrived in Jerusalem again, and as he was walking through the Temple area, the chief priests and other Jewish leaders came up to him demanding, "What's going on here? Who gave you the authority to drive out the merchants?"

[29] Jesus replied, "I'll tell you if you answer one question! [30] What about John the Baptist? Was he sent by God, or not? Answer me!"

[31] They talked it over among themselves. "If we reply that God sent him, then he will say, 'All right, why didn't you accept him?' [32] But if we say God

11:26 Many ancient authorities add vs 26, "but if you do not forgive, neither will your Father who is in heaven forgive your trespasses." All include this in Mt 6:15. **11:27** *other Jewish leaders*, literally, "scribes and elders." Also in 12:12.

11:17
Isa 56:7
Jer 7:11
11:18
Mt 21:46
Mk 12:12
Lk 4:32; 20:19
Jn 7:1

11:20
Mt 21:20–22

11:22
Mt 17:20
Lk 17:6

11:24
Mt 7:7
Lk 11:9
Jn 14:12–14; 15:7;
16:24
Jas 1:5–8
11:25
Mt 6:14, 15
Eph 4:32
Col 3:13

11:26
Mt 21:23–27
Lk 20:1–8

11:32
Mt 14:5
Mk 6:20

---

currency because this was the only money accepted for the Temple tax and for the purchase of animals for the sacrifices. Often the inflated exchange rate enriched the moneychangers, and the exorbitant prices of animals made the merchants wealthy. Their stalls were set up in the Court of the Gentiles in the Temple, frustrating the intentions of non-Jews who had come to worship God (Isaiah 56:6, 7). Jesus became angry because God's house of worship had become a place of extortion and a barrier to Gentiles who wanted to worship.

11:22, 23 The type of prayer about which Jesus spoke is the prayer for the fruitfulness of God's Kingdom. To pray a mountain of earth into the sea has nothing to do with God's will, but Jesus used that picture to say that it is possible for God to do the impossible. God answers prayer, but not as a result of a positive mental attitude. Other conditions must be met: (1) you must be a believer; (2) you must not hold a grudge against another person; (3) you must not pray with selfish motives. To pray effectively, you need faith in God, not faith in the object of your request. If you put your faith in your request, you will have nothing else your request is refused.

11:24 Jesus, our example for prayer, once prayed, "Everything is possible. . . . Yet I want your will, not

mine" (Mark 14:36). Often when we pray, we are motivated by our own interests and desires. We like to hear that we can have anything. But Jesus prayed with God's interests in mind. When we pray, we are to express our desires, but want his will above ours. Check yourself to see if your prayers are focusing on your interests or on God's.

11:26–30 The Pharisees asked Jesus who gave him the authority to chase away the merchants and moneychangers. Their request, however, was a trap. If Jesus said his authority was from God, they would accuse him of blasphemy; if he said his authority was his own, they would overrule him and dismiss him as a fanatic. To expose their real motives, Jesus countered their question with a question about John the Baptist. The Pharisees' silence proved they were not interested in the truth. They simply wanted to get rid of Jesus because he was undermining their authority. They did not base their lives on God, but on convenience—whatever served their own purposes at the time. Make sure your view of truth and justice is the same as God's, not whatever works for you at the moment.

11:30 For more information see John the Baptist's Profile in Mark 1.

didn't send him, then the people will start a riot." (For the people all believed strongly that John was a prophet.)

³³ So they said, "We can't answer. We don't know."

To which Jesus replied, "Then I won't answer your question either!"

11:33
Job 5:12, 13

Jesus tells the parable of the wicked farmers
(191/Matthew 21:33–46; Luke 20:9–19)

12 Here are some of the story-illustrations Jesus gave to the people at that time:

12:1
Isa 5:1, 2
Mt 21:33–46
Lk 20:9–19

"A man planted a vineyard and built a wall around it and dug a pit for pressing out the grape juice, and built a watchman's tower. Then he leased the farm to tenant farmers and moved to another country. ² At grape-picking time he sent one of his men to collect his share of the crop. ³ But the farmers beat up the man and sent him back empty-handed.

⁴ "The owner then sent another of his men, who received the same treatment, only worse, for his head was seriously injured. ⁵ The next man he sent was killed; and later, others were either beaten or killed, until ⁶ there was only one left—his only son. He finally sent him, thinking they would surely give him their full respect.

12:5
2 Chron 24:21
36:15, 16
Neh 9:26
Mt 23:34–37
Acts 7:52
1 Thess 2:15
12:6
Rom 8:3
Gal 4:4
12:7
Acts 4:27
12:8
Acts 2:23
12:9
Acts 28:23–29
12:10, 11
Ps 118:22, 23
Rom 9:33
Eph 2:20
1 Pet 2:5–7
12:12
Mt 11:18
Jn 7:26, 30, 44

⁷ "But when the farmers saw him coming they said, 'He will own the farm when his father dies. Come on, let's kill him—and then the farm will be ours!' ⁸ So they caught him and murdered him and threw his body out of the vineyard.

⁹ "What do you suppose the owner will do when he hears what happened? He will come and kill them all, and lease the vineyard to others. ¹⁰ Don't you remember reading this verse in the Scriptures? 'The Rock the builders threw away became the cornerstone, the most honored stone in the building! ¹¹ This is the Lord's doing and it is an amazing thing to see.' "

¹² The Jewish leaders wanted to arrest him then and there for using this illustration, for they knew he was pointing at them—they were the wicked farmers in his story. But they were afraid to touch him for fear of a mob. So they left him and went away.

Religious leaders question Jesus about paying taxes
(193/Matthew 22:15–22; Luke 20:20–26)

¹³ But they sent other religious and political leaders to talk with him and try to trap him into saying something he could be arrested for.

12:13
Mt 22:15–40, 46
Lk 20:20–40

12:1 The story-illustrations Jesus used are also called parables. A parable uses something familiar to help us understand something new. This method of teaching compels the listener to discover truth for himself. The message gets through only to those who are willing to listen and learn.

12:1ff In this parable, the landowner is God; the vineyard is the nation Israel; the farmers are the Jewish religious leaders; the landowner's men are the prophets and priests who remained faithful to God; the son is Jesus; the others are the Gentiles. By telling this story, Jesus let the religious leaders know he knew exactly what they were thinking, and he exposed their plot to kill him. He pointed out that their sins would not go unpunished.

12:1 Israel, pictured as a vineyard, was the place God had cultivated to bring salvation to the world. The nation's leaders not only frustrated the purpose of the vineyard, but they also killed those trying to take care of it. They were so jealous that they forgot the welfare of the very people they were supposed to be leading.

12:10 Jesus referred to himself as the Rock thrown away by the builders. Although he would be rejected by the Jews, he would become the cornerstone of a new "building," the church (Acts 4:11, 12). The cornerstone was used as a base to make sure the other stones of the building were straight and level. Likewise, Jesus' life and teaching would be the church's foundation, or base.

12:13 These religious and political leaders were the Pharisees and Herodians. The Pharisees were primarily a religious group; the Herodians, a Jewish political group.

The Pharisees did not like Jesus because he exposed their hypocrisy. The Herodians also saw Jesus as a threat. Supporters of the dynasty of Herod the Great, they had lost political control when, as a result of reported unrest, Rome deposed Herod's son and replaced him with a Roman governor. The Herodians feared that Jesus would cause still more instability in Judea, and that Rome might react by never allowing the Roman leaders to step down and be replaced by a descendant of Herod.

¹⁴"Teacher," these spies said, "we know you tell the truth no matter what! You aren't influenced by the opinions and desires of men, but sincerely teach the ways of God. Now tell us, is it right to pay taxes to Rome, or not?"

¹⁵Jesus saw their trick and said, "Show me a coin and I'll tell you."

¹⁶When they handed it to him he asked, "Whose picture and title is this on the coin?" They replied, "The emperor's."

¹⁷"All right," he said, "if it is his, give it to him. But everything that belongs to God must be given to God!" And they scratched their heads in bafflement at his reply.

Religious leaders question Jesus about the resurrection
(194/Matthew 22:23–32; Luke 20:27–40)

¹⁸Then the Sadducees stepped forward—a group of men who say there is no resurrection. Here was their question:

¹⁹"Teacher, Moses gave us a law that when a man dies without children, the man's brother should marry his widow and have children in his brother's name. ^{20, 21, 22}Well, there were seven brothers and the oldest married and died, and left no children. So the second brother married the widow, but soon he died too, and left no children. Then the next brother married her, and died without children, and so on until all were dead, and still there were no children; and last of all, the woman died too.

²³"What we want to know is this: In the resurrection, whose wife will she be, for she had been the wife of each of them?"

²⁴Jesus replied, "Your trouble is that you don't know the Scriptures, and don't know the power of God. ²⁵For when these seven brothers and the woman rise from the dead, they won't be married—they will be like the angels.

²⁶"But now as to whether there will be a resurrection—have you never read in the book of Exodus about Moses and the burning bush? God said to Moses,

12:23 *what we want to know is this,* implied.

12:18
Mt 22:23–33
Lk 20:27–38
Acts 23:8
1 Cor 15:12
12:19
Gen 38:8
Deut 25:5

12:24
Dan 12:2
Rom 4:17
1 Tim 1:7
2 Pet 1:19
12:25
1 Cor 15:42, 49, 52
1 Jn 3:2
12:26
Ex 3:6
Lk 20:37

12:14 Anyone avoiding taxes faced harsh penalties. The Jews hated to pay taxes to Rome because the money supported their oppressors and symbolized their subjection. Much of this tax also went to support the pagan temples and luxurious life-styles of Rome's upper class. The Pharisees and Herodians hoped to trap Jesus with this tax question. Either a yes or no could lead him into trouble. A yes would mean he supported Rome, which would turn the people against him. A no would bring accusations of treason and rebellion against Rome.

12:17 The Pharisees and Herodians thought they had the perfect question to trap Jesus. But Jesus answered wisely, once again exposing their self-interest and wrong motives. Jesus said that the coin bearing the emperor's image should be given to the emperor. But whatever bears God's image—our lives—belongs to God. Are you giving God all that is rightfully his? Make sure your life is given to God—you bear his image.

12:18 After the Pharisees and Herodians failed to trap Jesus with their tax question, the Sadducees stepped in with a question they were sure would stump Jesus. This was a question they had successfully used against the Pharisees, who could not come up with an answer. The Sadducees did not believe in life after death because the Pentateuch (Genesis—Deuteronomy) had no direct teaching about it, and those writings of Moses were the only Scriptures they followed. But Jesus was about to point out that Moses' books support the idea of eternal life (verse 26).

12:20–22 According to Old Testament law, when a woman's husband died without a son, the man's brother had to marry the woman in order to ensure children to care for the widow and allow the family line to continue. The first son of this marriage was considered the child of the dead man (Deuteronomy 25:5, 6).

12:24 Jesus said that not only were the Sadducees ignorant of Scripture, but they didn't understand God's power. Heaven is far beyond our ability to understand or imagine (Isaiah 64:4; 1 Corinthians 2:9). We must be careful not to create questions about heaven that cannot be answered from our human perspective. We need not be afraid of heaven because of the unknowns. Instead of wondering what God's coming Kingdom will be like, we should concentrate on our relationship with Jesus right now, because when we are in the new Kingdom we will be with him. How we live *now* will make a difference then.

12:25 Jesus' statement does not mean that a person will not recognize his or her partner in the coming Kingdom. It simply means that God's new order will not be an extension of this life—the same physical and natural rules won't apply. In our fallen world, relationships are limited by time, death, and human institutions, but in God's new and restored world they will not be.

12:26 Jesus answered their real question—"Will there be a resurrection?" Because the Sadducees believed only in the Pentateuch, Jesus quoted from Exodus 3:6 to prove that there is life after death. The Pharisees had overlooked this verse in their debates with the Sadducees over this issue. God spoke of Abraham, Isaac, and Jacob years after their death as if they *still lived.* God's covenant with all people exists beyond death.

'I *am* the God of Abraham, and I *am* the God of Isaac, and I *am* the God of Jacob.'

[27] "God was telling Moses that these men, though dead for hundreds of years, were still very much alive, for he would not have said, 'I *am* the God' of those who don't exist! You have made a serious error."

12:27
Mt 22:32
Lk 20:38

Religious leaders question Jesus about the greatest commandment (195/Matthew 22:33-40)

[28] One of the teachers of religion who was standing there listening to the discussion realized that Jesus had answered well. So he asked, "Of all the commandments, which is the most important?"

[29] Jesus replied, "The one that says, 'Hear, O Israel! The Lord our God is the one and only God. [30] And you must love him with all your heart and soul and mind and strength.'

[31] "The second is: 'You must love others as much as yourself.' No other commandments are greater than these."

12:29
Deut 6:4, 5
12:30
Lk 10:27
12:31
Lev 19:18
Rom 13:9
Gal 5:14
Jas 2:8

12:27 *though dead for hundreds of years,* implied.

What else did Jesus say about love?	*Reference*	**WHAT JESUS SAID ABOUT LOVE**
God loves us.	John 3:16	In Mark 12:28 a teacher of religion asked Jesus which of all the commandments was the most important to follow. Jesus mentioned two commandments, one from Deuteronomy 6:5, the other from Leviticus 19:18. Both had to do with love. Why is love so important? Jesus said that all of the commandments were given for two simple reasons—to help us love God and love others as we should.
We are to love God.	Matthew 22:37	
Because God loves us, he cares for us.	Matthew 6:25-34	
God wants everyone to know how much he loves them.	John 17:23	
God loves even those who hate him; we are to do the same.	Matthew 5:43-47; Luke 6:35	
God seeks out even those most alienated from him.	Luke 15	
God must be your first love.	Matthew 6:24; 10:37	
You love God when you obey him.	John 14:21; 15:10	
God loves Jesus his Son.	John 5:20; 10:17	
Jesus loves God.	John 14:31	
Those who refuse Jesus don't have God's love.	John 5:41-44	
Jesus loves us just as God loves Jesus.	John 15:9	
Jesus proved his love for us by dying on the cross so that we could live eternally with him.	John 3:14, 15; 15:13, 14	
The love between God and Jesus is the perfect example of how we are to love others.	John 17:21-26	
We are to love one another (John 13:34, 35) and demonstrate that love.	Matthew 5:40-42; 10:42	
We are *not* to love the praise of men (John 12:43), selfish recognition (Matthew 23:6), earthly belongings (Luke 16:19-31), or anything more than God.	Luke 16:13	
Jesus' love extends to each individual.	John 10:11-15; Mark 10:21	
Jesus wants us to love him through the good and difficult times.	Matthew 26:31-35	
Jesus wants our love to be genuine.	John 21:15-17	

12:28 By Jesus' time, the Jews had accumulated hundreds of laws—613, by one count. Some religious leaders tried to distinguish between major and minor laws, and some taught that all laws were equally binding and that it was dangerous to make any distinctions. This teacher's question could have provoked controversy among these groups, but Jesus' answer summarized all of God's laws.

12:29-31 God's laws are not burdensome in number or detail. They can be reduced to two simple rules for life:

love God, and love others. These commands are from the Old Testament (Leviticus 19:18; Deuteronomy 6:5). When you love God completely and care for others as you care for yourself, then you have fulfilled the intent of the Ten Commandments and the other Old Testament laws. According to Jesus, these two rules summarize all God's laws. Let them rule your thoughts, decisions, and actions. When you are uncertain about what to do, ask yourself which course of action best demonstrates love for God and love for others.

12:32
Deut 4:35, 39
Isa 45:5, 6, 14
46:9
1 Cor 8:4–6

12:33
1 Sam 15:22
Hos 6:6
Mic 6:6–8

12:34
Mt 22:46
Lk 14:6; 20:40

32 The teacher of religion replied, "Sir, you have spoken a true word in saying that there is only one God and no other. 33 And I know it is far more important to love him with all my heart and understanding and strength, and to love others as myself, than to offer all kinds of sacrifices on the altar of the Temple."

34 Realizing this man's understanding, Jesus said to him, "You are not far from the Kingdom of God." And after that, no one dared ask him any more questions.

Religious leaders cannot answer Jesus' question
(196/Matthew 22:41–46; Luke 20:41–44)

12:35
Mt 22:41–46
Lk 20:41–44

12:36
2 Sam 23:2
Ps 110:1
1 Cor 15:25
Heb 1:13
2 Pet 1:21

12:37
Rom 1:3; 9:5
Rev 22:16

35 Later, as Jesus was teaching the people in the Temple area, he asked them this question:

"Why do your religious teachers claim that the Messiah must be a descendant of King David? 36 For David himself said—and the Holy Spirit was speaking through him when he said it—'God said to my Lord, sit at my right hand until I make your enemies your footstool.' 37 Since David called him his Lord, how can he be his *son?*"

(This sort of reasoning delighted the crowd and they listened to him with great interest.)

Jesus warns against the religious leaders
(197/Matthew 23:1–12; Luke 20:45–47)

12:38
Mt 23:1–10, 14
Lk 20:45–47

12:39
Lk 11:43

38 Here are some of the other things he taught them at this time:

"Beware of the teachers of religion! For they love to wear the robes of the rich and scholarly, and to have everyone bow to them as they walk through the markets. 39 They love to sit in the best seats in the synagogues, and at the places of honor at banquets— 40 but they shamelessly cheat widows out of their homes and then, to cover up the kind of men they really are, they pretend to be pious by praying long prayers in public. Because of this, their punishment will be the greater."

A poor widow gives all she has
(200/Luke 21:1–4)

12:41
2 Kgs 12:9
Lk 21:1–4
Jn 8:20

41 Then he went over to the collection boxes in the Temple and sat and watched as the crowds dropped in their money. Some who were rich put in

---

12:33, 34 All the commands in the Old Testament lead to Christ. This man had caught the intent of God's law as it is so often stressed in the Old Testament—that heartfelt love is better than outward compliance, or that "obedience is better than sacrifice" (1 Samuel 15:22). His next step was faith in Jesus himself, and this was the most difficult step to take.

12:35, 36 Jesus quoted Psalm 110:1 to show that the Messiah would be different from an ordinary man. The religious leaders did not understand that the Messiah would be far more than a human descendant of David; he would be God himself in human form.

12:38-40 Jesus again exposed the Pharisees' impure motives. These religious leaders received no pay, so they depended upon the hospitality extended by devout Jews. Some of them used this custom to exploit people, cheating the poor out of everything they had and taking advantage of the rich. They acted spiritual to gain status, recognition, and respect.

12:38-40 Jesus warned against the teachers of religion who loved to appear holy and receive honor when, in reality, they were phonies. True followers of Christ are not distinguished by showy acts. Reading the Bible, praying in

public, or following church rituals can be phony if the motive for doing them is to be noticed or honored. Let your actions be consistent with your beliefs. You must live for Christ, even when no one is looking.

12:40 The punishment of the religious leaders would be greater because, as teachers and leaders, they carried great responsibility in shaping the faith of those they taught. But they saddled people with petty rules while forgetting the God they were supposed to worship, and their greed and impure motives led many people astray.

12:41 There were several boxes in the Temple where money could be placed. Some were for the collection of the Temple tax from Jewish males; the others were for free-will offerings. These particular collection boxes were probably in the Court of Women.

12:41-44 In the Lord's eyes, this poor widow gave more than all the others put together, although her gift was by far the smallest. The value of a gift is not determined by its amount, but by the spirit in which it is given. A gift given grudgingly or for recognition loses its value. When you give, take heart—small gifts are more pleasing to God than large gifts when they are given out of gratitude and generosity.

large amounts. ⁴²Then a poor widow came and dropped in two pennies.

⁴³, ⁴⁴He called his disciples to him and remarked, "That poor widow has given more than all those rich men put together! For they gave a little of their extra fat, while she gave up her last penny."

12:43
Lk 8:43, 44
2 Cor 8:12

Jesus tells about the future
(201/Matthew 24:1–22; Luke 21:5–24)

13 As he was leaving the Temple that day, one of his disciples said, "Teacher, what beautiful buildings these are! Look at the decorated stonework on the walls."

13:1
Mt 24:1–51
Lk 21:5–36

²Jesus replied, "Yes, look! For not one stone will be left upon another, except as ruins."

13:2
Lk 19:43, 44

³, ⁴And as he sat on the slopes of the Mount of Olives across the valley from Jerusalem, Peter, James, John, and Andrew got alone with him and asked him, "Just when is all this going to happen to the Temple? Will there be some warning ahead of time?

⁵So Jesus launched into an extended reply. "Don't let anyone mislead you," he said, ⁶"for many will come declaring themselves to be your Messiah,

12:43, 44 *a little of their extra fat,* literally, "out of their surplus."

Type of Prophecy	Old Testament References	Other New Testament References	**JESUS' PROPHECIES IN THE OLIVET DISCOURSE**
The Last Days Mark 13:1–23 Matthew 24:1–28 Luke 21:5–24	Daniel 9:26 27 Daniel 11:31 Joel 2:2	John 15:21 Revelation 11:2 1 Timothy 4:1, 2	
The Second Coming of Christ Mark 13:24–27 Luke 21:25–28 Matthew 24:29–31	Isaiah 13:6–10 Ezekiel 32:7 Daniel 7:13, 14	Revelation 6:12 Mark 14:62 1 Thessalonians 4:16	

In Mark 13, often called the Olivet Discourse, Jesus talked a lot about two things: the end times and his Second Coming. Jesus was not trying to encourage his disciples to speculate about exactly when he would return by sharing these prophecies with them. Instead, he urges all his followers to be watchful and prepared for his coming. If we serve Jesus faithfully now, we will be ready when he returns.

13:1, 2 About fifteen years before Jesus was born (20 B.C.) Herod the Great began to remodel and rebuild the Temple, which had stood for nearly five hundred years, since the days of Ezra (Ezra 6:14, 15). Herod made the Temple one of the most beautiful buildings in Jerusalem, not to honor God, but to appease the Jews whom he ruled. The magnificent building project was not completely finished until A.D. 64. Jesus' prophecy that not one stone would be left upon another was fulfilled in A.D. 70, when the Romans completely destroyed the Temple and the entire city of Jerusalem.

13:3ff The disciples wanted to know when the Temple would be destroyed. Jesus gave them a prophetic picture of that time, including events leading up to it. He also talked about other future events which would signal his return. Jesus predicted both near and distant events without trying to put them in chronological order. The disciples lived to see the destruction of Jerusalem in A.D. 70. This event would assure them that everything else Jesus predicted would also happen.

Jesus warned them about the future so that they could learn how to live in the present. Many predictions Jesus made in this passage have not yet been fulfilled. He did not make them so that we would guess when they might happen, but to help us remain spiritually alert and prepared at all times, waiting for his return.

13:3, 4 The Mount of Olives rises above Jerusalem to the east of the city. From its slopes a person can look down into the city and see the Temple. Zechariah 14:1–4 predicts that the Messiah will stand on this very mountain when he returns to set up his eternal kingdom.

13:5–7 What are the signs of the end times? There have been people in every generation since Christ's resurrection claiming to know exactly when Jesus would return. No one has been right yet, however, because Christ will return on God's timetable, not man's. Jesus predicted that many believers would be misled before his return by false teachers claiming to have revelations from God.

In Scripture, the one clear sign of Christ's return is that all mankind will see him coming in the clouds (verse 26). In other words, you do not have to wonder whether a certain person is the Messiah or whether these are the "end times." When Jesus returns, *you will know* beyond a doubt. Beware of groups that claim special knowledge of the last days because no one knows when this time will be (verse 32). Be cautious about saying, "This is it!" but be bold in your total commitment to have your heart and life ready for his return.

and will lead many astray. [7] And wars will break out near and far, but this is not the signal of the end-time.

[8] "For nations and kingdoms will proclaim war against each other, and there will be earthquakes in many lands, and famines. These herald only the early stages of the anguish ahead. [9] But when these things begin to happen, watch out! For you will be in great danger. You will be dragged before the courts, and beaten in the synagogues, and accused before governors and kings of being my followers. This is your opportunity to tell them the Good News. [10] And the Good News must first be made known in every nation before the end-time finally comes. [11] But when you are arrested and stand trial, don't worry about what to say in your defense. Just say what God tells you to. Then you will not be speaking, but the Holy Spirit will.

[12] "Brothers will betray each other to death, fathers will betray their own children, and children will betray their parents to be killed. [13] And everyone will hate you because you are mine. But all who endure to the end without renouncing me shall be saved.

[14] "When you see the horrible thing standing in the Temple—reader, pay attention!—flee, if you can, to the Judean hills. [15, 16] Hurry! If you are on your rooftop porch, don't even go back into the house. If you are out in the fields, don't even return for your money or clothes.

[17] "Woe to pregnant women in those days, and to mothers nursing their children. [18] And pray that your flight will not be in winter. [19] For those will be days of such horror as have never been since the beginning of God's creation, nor will ever be again. [20] And unless the Lord shortens that time of calamity, not a soul in all the earth will survive. But for the sake of his chosen ones he will limit those days.

Jesus tells about his return
(202/Matthew 24:23-35; Luke 21:25-33)

[21] "And then if anyone tells you, 'This is the Messiah,' or, 'That one is,' don't pay any attention. [22] For there will be many false Messiahs and false prophets who will do wonderful miracles that would deceive, if possible, even God's own children. [23] Take care! I have warned you!

13:10 *before the end-time finally comes,* implied. **13:14** *standing in the Temple,* literally, ''standing where he ought not.'' **13:22** *God's own children,* literally, the ''elect of God.''

Cross-references (left margin):
13:9 Mt 10:17-22
13:10 Rom 10:18
13:11 Lk 12:11, 12; 21:14, 15 Acts 2:4; 4:8, 31
13:12 Mic 7:6
13:13 Jn 15:18-21 2 Tim 4:7, 8 Heb 3:6, 14 Rev 2:10
13:14 Dan 9:27 11:31; 12:11 Mt 24:15
13:17 Lk 23:29
13:19 Jer 30:7 Dan 12:1 Joel 2:2 Rev 3:10
13:21 Lk 17:23
13:22 Mt 7:15; 24:24 2 Thess 2:9
13:23 2 Pet 3:17

13:9, 10 As the early church began to grow, most of the disciples experienced the kind of persecution Jesus was talking about. Since the time of Christ, Christians have been persecuted in their own lands and on foreign mission fields. Though you may be safe from persecution now, your vision of God's Kingdom must not be limited by what happens only to you. A quick look at a newspaper will show you that many Christians in other parts of the world daily face hardships and persecution. Persecutions are an opportunity for Christians to witness for Christ to those opposed to him. They serve God's desire that the Good News be made available to everyone.

13:11 Jesus is not saying that studying the Bible and gaining knowledge are useless or wrong. Before and after his resurrection Jesus himself taught his disciples what to say and how to say it. But Jesus is telling us what attitude we can have when we must take a stand for the gospel. We don't have to be fearful or defensive about our faith because the Holy Spirit will be present to give us the right words to say.

13:13 To believe in Jesus ''to the end'' will take perseverance because our faith will be challenged and opposed. These trials will sift true Christians from fair-weather believers. Enduring to the end does not earn salvation for us, but marks us as those already saved. The assurance of our salvation will keep us going in the midst of persecution.

13:14 The ''horrible thing'' Jesus mentioned is the desecration of the Temple by those who insult God's holiness. In A.D. 38, the emperor Caligula planned to put his own statue in the Temple, but he died before his plans were carried out. In A.D. 70, the emperor Titus placed an idol on the site of the burned-out Temple after the destruction of Jerusalem.

13:22, 23 Is it possible for Christians to be deceived? Yes. So convincing will be the arguments and proofs from deceivers in the end times that it will be difficult *not* to fall away from Christ. If we are prepared, Jesus says, we can remain faithful, but if we are not prepared we will not endure. To penetrate the disguises of false teachers we can ask: (1) Have their predictions come true, or do they have to revise them to fit what's already happened? (2) Does any teaching utilize a small section of the Bible to the neglect of the whole? (3) Does the teaching go against what is said in the Bible about God? (4) Are the practices meant to glorify the teacher or Christ? (5) Do the teachings promote hostility toward other Christians?

²⁴"After the tribulation ends, then the sun will grow dim and the moon will not shine, ²⁵ and the stars will fall—the heavens will convulse.

²⁶"Then all mankind will see me, the Messiah, coming in the clouds with great power and glory. ²⁷ And I will send out the angels to gather together my chosen ones from all over the world—from the farthest bounds of earth and heaven.

²⁸"Now, here is a lesson from a fig tree. When its buds become tender and its leaves begin to sprout, you know that spring has come. ²⁹ And when you see these things happening that I've described, you can be sure that my return is very near, that I am right at the door.

³⁰"Yes, these are the events that will signal the end of the age. ³¹ Heaven and earth shall disappear, but my words stand sure forever.

Jesus tells about remaining watchful
(203/Matthew 24:36–51; Luke 21:34–38)

³²"However, no one, not even the angels in heaven, nor I myself, knows the day or hour when these things will happen; only the Father knows. ³³ And since you don't know when it will happen, stay alert. Be on the watch [for my return].

³⁴"My coming can be compared with that of a man who went on a trip to another country. He laid out his employees' work for them to do while he was gone, and told the gatekeeper to watch for his return.

³⁵, ³⁶, ³⁷"Keep a sharp lookout! For you do not know when I will come, at evening, at midnight, early dawn or late daybreak. Don't let me find you sleeping. *Watch for my return!* This is my message to you and to everyone else."

C. DEATH AND RESURRECTION OF JESUS, THE SERVANT (14:1—16:20)

Mark tells us about Jesus' ultimate deed of servanthood—dying for us on the cross. Jesus died for our sin so we wouldn't have to. Now we can have eternal fellowship with God instead of eternal suffering and death. When first written in Rome, this Gospel was encouraging to Roman Christians during times of persecution. Christ's victory through suffering can encourage us during difficult times too.

13:26 *the Messiah,* literally, "the Son of Man." **13:30** *of the age,* literally, "of this generation." **13:32** *I myself,* literally, "the Son." **13:33** *for my return,* implied. **13:34** *My coming,* literally, "You do not know when the master of the house will come." **13:35-37** *I,* implied.

Cross-references:
13:24 Isa 13:10; Ezek 32:7, 8; Joel 2:31; 3:15; Zech 1:15; Acts 2:20; Rev 6:12
13:26 Dan 7:13; Mt 16:27; Acts 1:11; 1 Thess 4:16; 2 Thess 1:7; Rev 1:7
13:27 Deut 30:3, 4
13:31 Isa 40:8; 51:6; Ps 102:25–27
13:32 Acts 1:7
13:33 Rom 13:11; Eph 6:17, 18; Col 4:2; 1 Thess 5:6
13:34 Mt 25:14; Lk 19:9
13:35–37 Lk 12:39, 40; 2 Pet 3:1–18; Rev 3:3

13:31 In Jesus' day the world seemed very concrete and dependable, giving the impression of permanence. Nowadays many people fear its destruction by nuclear power. Jesus tells us, however, that while we can be sure the earth will pass away, the truth of his words will never be changed or abolished. God and his Word provide the only stability in our unstable world. How shortsighted to spend so much of our time learning about this temporary world and accumulating its possessions, while neglecting the Bible and its eternal truths.

13:32 When Jesus said that even he did not know the time of the end, he was affirming his humanity. Of course God the Father knows the time, and Jesus and the Father are one, but when Jesus became a man, he voluntarily gave up the unlimited use of his divine attributes. The emphasis of this verse is not on Jesus' lack of knowledge, but rather on the fact that no one knows. It is God the Father's secret to be revealed when he wills. No one can predict by Scripture or science the exact day of Jesus' return. Jesus is teaching that preparation, not calculation is needed.

13:33, 34 Months of planning go into a wedding, the birth of a baby, a career change, a speaking engagement, the purchase of a home. Do we place the same importance on preparing for Christ's return? His return is the most important event in our lives. Its results will last for eternity. You dare not postpone preparing for it because you do not know when it will occur. The only way to prepare is to study God's Word and then determine to live by its instructions each day. Only then will you be ready.

13:35 This entire passage (verses 3–37) tells us how to live while we wait for Christ's return: (1) We are not to be misled by confusing claims or idle interpretations of what will happen (verses 5, 6). (2) We should not be afraid to tell anyone about Christ, despite what they might say or do to us (verses 9–11). (3) We must endure by faith and not be surprised by persecutions (verse 13). (4) We must be morally alert and obedient to the commands for living found in God's Word. This chapter was not given to promote discussions on events in prophecy, but to stimulate talk about right living for God in a world where God is largely ignored.

Religious leaders plot to kill Jesus
(207/Matthew 26:1–5; Luke 22:1, 2)

14:1
Mt 26:1–5
Lk 22:1, 2
Jn 11:55–57

14 The Passover observance began two days later—an annual Jewish holiday when no bread made with yeast was eaten. The chief priests and other Jewish leaders were still looking for an opportunity to arrest Jesus secretly and put him to death.

2 "But we can't do it during the Passover," they said, "or there will be a riot."

A woman anoints Jesus with perfume
(182/Matthew 26:6–13; John 12:1–11)

14:3
Mt 26:6–13
Lk 7:37–39
Jn 12:1–8

3 Meanwhile Jesus was in Bethany, at the home of Simon the leper; during supper a woman came in with a beautiful flask of expensive perfume. Then, breaking the seal, she poured it over his head.

4, 5 Some of those at the table were indignant among themselves about this "waste," as they called it.

"Why, she could have sold that perfume for a fortune and given the money to the poor!" they snarled.

14:7
Deut 15:11

6 But Jesus said, "Let her alone; why berate her for doing a good thing? 7 You always have the poor among you, and they badly need your help, and you can aid them whenever you want to; but I won't be here much longer.

14:8
Mk 16:1
Lk 24:1
Jn 19:40

8 "She has done what she could, and has anointed my body ahead of time for burial. 9 And I tell you this in solemn truth, that wherever the Good News is preached throughout the world, this woman's deed will be remembered and praised."

Judas agrees to betray Jesus
(208/Matthew 26:14–16; Luke 22:3–6)

14:10
Mt 26:14–16
Lk 22:3–6
Jn 6:71

10 Then Judas Iscariot, one of his disciples, went to the chief priests to arrange to betray Jesus to them.

14:1 For the festival of the Passover, all Jewish males over 12 years of age were required to go to Jerusalem. The Passover commemorated the night the Israelites were freed from Egypt (Exodus 12) when God "passed over" homes marked by the blood of a lamb while killing firstborn sons in unmarked homes. The Day of Passover was followed by a seven-day festival called the Feast of Unleavened Bread. This, too, recalled the Israelites' quick escape from Egypt when they didn't have time to let their bread rise, so they baked it without yeast. This Jewish holiday found people gathering for a special meal that included lamb, wine, bitter meats, and unleavened bread. Eventually the whole week came to be called Passover because it immediately followed the special Passover holiday.

14:1 The Jewish leaders plotted secretly to kill Jesus— his murder was carefully planned. It was not because popular opinion had turned against him. In fact, the leaders were afraid of Jesus' popularity.

14:3 Bethany is located on the eastern slope of the Mount of Olives (Jerusalem is on the western side). This town was the home of Jesus' friends Lazarus, Mary, and Martha, who were also present at this dinner (John 11:17). The woman who anointed Jesus' feet was Mary, Lazarus' and Martha's sister (John 12:1–3).

14:3–9 Matthew and Mark placed this event just before the Last Supper, while John placed it a week earlier, just before the Triumphal Entry. It must be remembered that the main purpose of the Gospel writers was not to present an exact chronological account of Christ's life, but to give

an accurate record of his message. Matthew and Mark may have chosen to place this event here to contrast the complete devotion of Mary with the betrayal of Judas, the next event in both Gospels.

14:4, 5 Where Mark says "some of those at the table," John specifically mentions Judas (John 12:4). Judas' indignation over Mary's act of worship was not out of concern for the poor but out of greed. Since he was the treasurer of Jesus' ministry and had embezzled funds (John 12:6), he no doubt wanted the perfume sold so that the proceeds could be put into his care.

14:6 Jesus was not saying that we should neglect the poor, nor was he justifying indifference to them. He was praising Mary for her unselfish act of worship. The essence of worshiping Christ is to regard him with utmost love, respect, and devotion and to be willing to sacrifice to him what is most precious.

14:10 Why would Judas want to betray Jesus? Judas, like the other disciples, expected Jesus to start a political rebellion and overthrow Rome. As treasurer, Judas certainly assumed (as did the other disciples—see 10:35–37) that he would be given an important position in Jesus' new government. But when Jesus praised Mary for pouring out the perfume, thought to be worth half a year's salary, Judas finally realized that Jesus' kingdom was not physical or political, but spiritual. Judas' greedy desire for money and status could not be realized if he followed Jesus, so he betrayed him in exchange for money and favor from the religious leaders.

11 When the chief priests heard why he had come, they were excited and happy and promised him a reward. So he began looking for the right time and place to betray Jesus.

14:11
Zech 11:12
1 Tim 6:10
Jude 11

Disciples prepare for the Passover
(209/Matthew 26:17–19; Luke 22:7–13)

12 On the first day of the Passover, the day the lambs were sacrificed, his disciples asked him where he wanted to go to eat the traditional Passover

14:12
Deut 16:5
Mt 26:17–19
Lk 22:7–13
1 Cor 5:7, 8

Day	Event	References	MAJOR EVENTS OF PASSION WEEK
Sunday	Triumphal entry into Jerusalem	Matthew 21:1–11 Mark 11:1–10 Luke 19:29–40 John 12:12–19	Sunday through Wednesday Jesus spent each night in Bethany, just two miles east of Jerusalem on the
Monday	Jesus cleanses the Temple	Matthew 21:12, 13 Mark 11:15–17 Luke 19:45, 46	opposite slope of the Mount of Olives. He
Tuesday	Jesus' authority challenged in the Temple	Matthew 21:23–27 Mark 11:26–33 Luke 20:1–8	probably stayed at the home of Mary, Martha, and
	Jesus teaches in stories and confronts the Jewish leaders	Matthew 21:28—23:36 Mark 12:1–40 Luke 20:9–47	Lazarus. Jesus spent Thursday night praying in
	Greeks ask to see Jesus	John 12:20–26	the Garden of Gethsemane.
	The Olivet Discourse	Matthew 24 Mark 13 Luke 21:5–38	Friday and Saturday nights Jesus' body lay in
	Judas agrees to betray Jesus	Matthew 26:14–16 Mark 14:10, 11 Luke 22:3–6	the Garden Tomb.
Wednesday	The Bible does not say what Jesus did on this day. He probably remained in Bethany with his disciples		
Thursday	The Last Supper	Matthew 26:26–29 Mark 14:22–25 Luke 22:14–20	
	Jesus speaks to the disciples in the Upper Room	John 13—17	
	Jesus struggles in Gethsemane	Matthew 26:36–46 Mark 14:32–42 Luke 22:39–46 John 18:1	
	Jesus is betrayed and arrested	Matthew 26:47–56 Mark 14:43–52 Luke 22:47–53 John 18:2–12	
Friday	Jesus is tried by Jewish and Roman authorities and denied by Peter	Matthew 26:57—27:2, 11–31 Mark 14:53—15:20 Luke 22:54—23:25 John 18:13—19:16	
	Jesus is crucified	Matthew 27:31–56 Mark 15:20–41 Luke 23:26–49 John 19:17–30	
Sunday	The resurrection	Matthew 28:1–10 Mark 16:1–11 Luke 24:1–12 John 20:1–18	

JUDAS ISCARIOT

It is easy to overlook the fact that Jesus chose Judas to be his disciple. We may also forget that while Judas betrayed Jesus, *all* the disciples abandoned him. With the other disciples, Judas shared a persistent misunderstanding of Jesus' mission. They all expected Jesus to make the right political moves. When he kept talking about dying, they all felt varying degrees of anger, fear, and disappointment. They didn't understand why they had been chosen if Jesus' mission was doomed to fail.

We do not know the exact motivation behind Judas' betrayal. What is clear is that Judas allowed his desires to place him in a position where Satan could manipulate him. He got paid to set Jesus up for the religious leaders. He identified Jesus for the guards in the dimly lit garden of Gethsemane. It is possible that he was trying to force Jesus' hand—would he or would he not rebel against Rome and set up a new political government?

Whatever his plan, though, at some point Judas realized he didn't like the way things were turning out. He tried to undo the evil he had done by returning the money to the priests, but it was too late. The wheels of God's sovereign plan had been set into motion. How sad that Judas ended his life in despair without ever experiencing the gift of reconciliation God could give even to him through Jesus Christ.

Human feelings toward Judas have always been mixed. Some have fervently hated him for his betrayal. Others have pitied him for not realizing what he was doing. A few have tried to make him a hero for his part in ending Jesus' earthly mission. Some have questioned God's fairness in allowing one man to bear such guilt. While there are many feelings about Judas, there are some facts to consider as well. He, by his own choice, betrayed God's Son into the hands of Roman soldiers (Luke 22:48). He was a thief (John 12:6). Jesus knew that Judas' life of evil would not change (John 6:70). Judas' betrayal of Jesus was part of God's sovereign plan (Psalm 41:9; Zechariah 11:12, 13; Matthew 20:18; 26:20–25; Acts 1:16, 20).

In betraying Jesus, Judas made the greatest mistake in history. But just the fact that Jesus knew Judas would betray him doesn't mean that Judas was a puppet of God's will. Judas made the choice. God knew what that choice would be and confirmed it. Judas didn't lose his relationship with Jesus; rather, he had never found Jesus. He is called the "son of hell" (John 17:12) because he was never saved.

Judas does us a favor if he makes us think a second time about our committment to God and the presence of his Spirit within us. Are we true disciples and followers, or uncommitted pretenders? We can choose despair and death, or we can choose repentance, forgiveness, hope, and eternal life. Judas' betrayal sent Jesus to the cross to guarantee that second choice, our only chance. Will we accept his free gift, or like Judas, betray him?

Strengths and accomplishments:
- He was chosen as one of the twelve disciples; the only non-Galilean
- He kept the money bag for the expenses of the group
- He was able to recognize the evil in his betrayal of Jesus

Weaknesses and mistakes:
- He was greedy (John 12:6)
- He betrayed Jesus
- He committed suicide instead of seeking forgiveness

Lessons from his life:
- Evil plans and motives leave us open to being used by Satan for even greater evil
- The consequences of evil are so devastating that even small lies and little wrongdoings have serious results
- God's plan and his purposes are worked out even in the worst possible events

Key verse:
"Then Satan entered into Judas Iscariot, who was one of the twelve disciples, and he went over to the chief priests and captains of the Temple guards to discuss the best way to betray Jesus to them" (Luke 22:3, 4).

Vital statistics:
Where: probably from the town of Kerioth
Occupation: disciple of Jesus
Relatives: Father, Simon.
Contemporaries: Jesus, Pilate, Herod, the other 11 disciples.

Judas' story is told in the Gospels. He is also mentioned in Acts 1:18, 19.

supper. [13] He sent two of them into Jerusalem to make the arrangements.

"As you are walking along," he told them, "you will see a man coming toward you carrying a pot of water. Follow him. [14] At the house he enters, tell the man in charge, 'Our Master sent us to see the room you have ready for us, where we will eat the Passover supper this evening!' [15] He will take you upstairs to a large room all set up. Prepare our supper there."

[16] So the two disciples went on ahead into the city and found everything as Jesus had said, and prepared the Passover.

14:14
Ex 12:8
Lev 23:5

Jesus and the disciples have the Last Supper
(211/Matthew 26:20–29; Luke 22:14–30; John 13:21–30)

[17] In the evening Jesus arrived with the other disciples, [18] and as they were sitting around the table eating, Jesus said, "I solemnly declare that one of you will betray me, one of you who is here eating with me."

14:17
Mt 26:20–30
Lk 22:14–23
Jn 13:21–30

[19] A great sadness swept over them, and one by one they asked him, "Am I the one?"

[20] He replied, "It is one of you twelve eating with me now. [21] I must die, as the prophets declared long ago; but, oh, the misery ahead for the man by whom I am betrayed. Oh, that he had never been born!"

14:21
Ps 22:1–21
Isa 53:3–8

[22] As they were eating, Jesus took bread and asked God's blessing on it and broke it in pieces and gave it to them and said, "Eat it—this is my body."

14:22
1 Cor 10:16
11:23–26

[23] Then he took a cup of wine and gave thanks to God for it and gave it to them; and they all drank from it. [24] And he said to them, "This is my blood,

14:24
Heb 9:13–15

14:21 *I*, literally, "the Son of Man." **14:24** *sealing*, literally, "This is my blood of the covenant." Some ancient manuscripts read "new covenant."

14:13 The two men Jesus sent were Peter and John (Luke 22:8).

14:14, 15 Many homes had large upstairs rooms, sometimes with stairways both inside and outside the house. The preparations for the Passover would have included setting the table and buying and preparing the Passover lamb, unleavened bread, sauces, and other ceremonial food and drink.

14:19 Judas, the very man who would betray Jesus, was at the table with the others. He had already determined to betray Jesus, but in cold-blooded hypocrisy he shared the fellowship of this meal. It is easy to become enraged or shocked by what Judas did, yet when we profess commitment to Christ and then deny him with our lives we also betray him. We deny Christ's truth because he taught us how to live and we live otherwise. We deny Christ's love by not obeying him. And we deny Christ's deity by rejecting his authority. Do your words and actions match? If not, consider a change of mind and heart that will protect you from making a terrible mistake.

14:22-25 Mark records the origin of the Lord's Supper, also called Communion or Eucharist, which is still celebrated in worship services today. Jesus and his disciples ate a meal, sang Psalms, read Scripture, and prayed. Then Jesus took two traditional parts of the Passover meal, the passing of bread and the drinking of wine, and gave them new meaning as his body and blood. He used the bread and wine to explain the significance of what he was about to do on the cross. For more on the significance of the Last Supper, see 1 Corinthians 11:23-29.

14:24 Jesus' death for us on the cross seals a new agreement between God and mankind. The old agreement involved forgiveness of sins through the blood of an animal sacrifice (Exodus 24:6-8). But, instead of a spotless lamb on the altar, Jesus came as the Lamb of God to sacrifice himself to forgive sin once and for all.

Jesus was the final sacrifice for sins, and his blood sealed the new agreement between God and us (also called the "new covenant" or "new testament"). Now all of us can come to God through Jesus, in full confidence that he will hear us and save us from our sins.

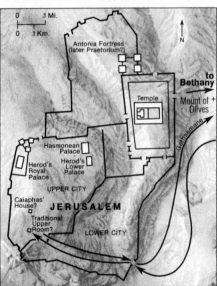

UPPER ROOM AND GETHSEMANE Jesus and the disciples ate the traditional Passover meal in an upper room in the city and then went to the Mount of Olives into a garden called Gethsemane. In the cool of the evening, Jesus prayed for strength to face the trial and suffering ahead.

poured out for many, sealing the new agreement between God and man. ²⁵ I solemnly declare that I shall never again taste wine until the day I drink a different kind in the Kingdom of God."

Jesus again predicts Peter's denial
(222/Matthew 26:30–35)

²⁶ Then they sang a hymn and went out to the Mount of Olives.

14:27
Zech 13:7
Mt 26:31–35
Lk 22:31–34
Jn 13:36–38

²⁷ "All of you will desert me," Jesus told them, "for God has declared through the prophets, 'I will kill the Shepherd, and the sheep will scatter.'

14:28
Mk 16:7

²⁸ But after I am raised to life again, I will go to Galilee and meet you there."

²⁹ Peter said to him, "I will never desert you no matter what the others do!"

³⁰ "Peter," Jesus said, "before the cock crows a second time tomorrow morning you will deny me three times."

³¹ "No!" Peter exploded. "Not even if I have to die with you! I'll *never* deny you!" And all the others vowed the same.

Jesus agonizes in the garden
(223/Matthew 26:36–46; Luke 22:39–46)

14:32
Mt 26:36–46
Lk 22:39–46
Jn 18:1

³² And now they came to an olive grove called the Garden of Gethsemane, and he instructed his disciples, "Sit here, while I go and pray."

14:33
Mt 17:1
Mk 9:2
Lk 9:28

³³ He took Peter, James and John with him and began to be filled with horror and deepest distress. ³⁴ And he said to them, "My soul is crushed by sorrow to the point of death; stay here and watch with me."

14:35
Jn 12:27
Heb 5:7

³⁵ He went on a little further and fell to the ground and prayed that if it were possible the awful hour awaiting him might never come.

14:36
Mt 20:22
Jn 5:30; 6:38; 18:11
Rom 8:15
Gal 4:6

³⁶ "Father, Father," he said, "everything is possible for you. Take away this cup from me. Yet I want your will, not mine."

³⁷ Then he returned to the three disciples and found them asleep.

"Simon!" he said. "Asleep? Couldn't you watch with me even one hour?

14:38
Rom 7:23
Gal 5:17

³⁸ Watch with me and pray lest the Tempter overpower you. For though the spirit is willing enough, the body is weak."

³⁹ And he went away again and prayed, repeating his pleadings. ⁴⁰ Again he returned to them and found them sleeping, for they were very tired. And they didn't know what to say.

⁴¹ The third time when he returned to them he said, "Sleep on; get your rest! But no! The time for sleep has ended! Look! I am betrayed into the hands of wicked men. ⁴² Come! Get up! We must go! Look! My betrayer is here!"

14:25 *drink a different kind,* literally, "drink it new." **14:35** *the awful hour . . . might never come,* literally, "that the hour might pass away from him." **14:41** *I,* literally, "the Son of Man."

14:26 The hymn they sang was most likely taken from Psalms 115—118, which were traditionally sung to conclude the Passover meal.

14:27 It's easy to think that Satan temporarily gained the upper hand in this drama about Jesus' death. But we see later that God is in control even in the death of his Son. Satan gained no victory—everything occurred exactly as God had planned.

14:27 This is the second time in the same evening that Jesus predicted the disciples' denial and desertion, which probably explains why they reacted so strongly (verse 31). For Jesus' earlier prediction of their denial see Luke 22:31–38 and John 13:31–38.

14:35, 36 Was Jesus trying to get out of his task? Jesus expressed his true feelings, but he did not deny or rebel against God's will. He reaffirmed his desire to do what God wanted. His prayer highlights the terrible suffering he had to endure—an agony worse than dying, because he had to take on the sins of the whole world. This "cup"

was the alienation Jesus knew would occur when he was separated from God, his Father, at the cross (Hebrews 5:7–9). The sinless Son of God took on our sins and was separated in that moment from God in order that we could be saved.

14:36–38 While praying, Jesus was aware of what doing the Father's will would cost him. He understood the suffering he was about to encounter, and he did not want to have to endure the horrible experience. But Christ prayed, "I want your will, not mine." What does your commitment to God cost you? Anything worth having costs something. Be willing to pay the price to have something worthwhile in the end.

14:41 In times of great stress we are vulnerable to temptation, even if we have a willing spirit. Jesus gave us an example of what to do to resist: (1) pray to God (verse 35); (2) seek support of friends and loved ones (verses 33, 37, 40, 41); (3) focus on the purpose God has given us (verse 36).

Jesus is betrayed and arrested
(224/Matthew 26:47–56; Luke 22:47–53; John 18:1–11)

⁴³ And immediately, while he was still speaking, Judas (one of his disciples) arrived with a mob equipped with swords and clubs, sent out by the chief priests and other Jewish leaders.

⁴⁴ Judas had told them, "You will know which one to arrest when I go over and greet him. Then you can take him easily. ⁴⁵ So as soon as they arrived he walked up to Jesus. "Master!" he exclaimed, and embraced him with a great show of friendliness. ⁴⁶ Then the mob arrested Jesus and held him fast. ⁴⁷ But someone pulled a sword and slashed at the High Priest's servant, cutting off his ear.

⁴⁸ Jesus asked them, "Am I some dangerous robber, that you come like this, armed to the teeth to capture me? ⁴⁹ Why didn't you arrest me in the Temple? I was there teaching every day. But these things are happening to fulfill the prophecies about me."

⁵⁰ Meanwhile, all his disciples had fled. ⁵¹, ⁵² There was, however, a young man following along behind, clothed only in a linen nightshirt. When the mob tried to grab him, he escaped, though his clothes were torn off in the process, so that he ran away completely naked.

Caiaphas questions Jesus
(226/Matthew 26:57–68)

⁵³ Jesus was led to the High Priest's home where all of the chief priests and other Jewish leaders soon gathered. ⁵⁴ Peter followed far behind and then slipped inside the gates of the High Priest's residence and crouched beside a fire among the servants.

14:43 Mt 26:47–56 / Lk 22:47–53 / Jn 18:2–11
14:45 Jn 20:16
14:47 Jn 18:10
14:49 Ps 22:6–18 / Isa 53:7–9 / Dan 9:26 / Lk 24:44
14:50 Ps 88:8 / Jn 16:32
14:53 Mt 26:57–68 / Lk 22:54, 63–71 / Jn 18:12–14, 19–24
14:54 Mt 26:3 / Jn 18:18

14:44 *greet*, literally, "kiss," the usual oriental greeting, even to this day. **14:51, 52** *in a linen nightshirt*, literally, "wearing only a linen cloth."

14:43–45 Judas was given a contingent of Jewish Temple police as well as some Roman soldiers (John 18:3) in order to seize Jesus and bring him before the religious court for trial. The religious leaders had issued the warrant for Jesus' arrest, and Judas was acting as Jesus' official accuser.

14:47 According to John 18:10, the person who pulled the sword was Peter. Luke 22:51 records that Jesus immediately healed the man's ear and prevented any further bloodshed.

14:50 Just hours earlier, these disciples had vowed never to desert Jesus (verse 31).

14:51, 52 Tradition says that this young man might have been John Mark, the writer of this Gospel. The incident is not mentioned in any of the other accounts.

14:53ff This trial by the Jewish Supreme Court had two phases. A small group met at night (John 18:12–24), and then the full council met at daybreak (Luke 22:66–71). They tried Jesus for religious offenses such as calling himself the Son of God, which, according to law, was blasphemy. The trial was obviously fixed, because these religious leaders had already decided to kill Jesus (Luke 22:2).

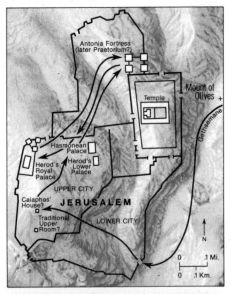

JESUS' TRIAL From Gethsemane, Jesus' trial began at the home of Caiaphas, the High Priest. He was then taken to Pilate, the Roman governor. Luke records that Pilate sent him to Herod, who was in Jerusalem—presumably in one of his two palaces (Luke 23:5–12). Herod sent Jesus back to Pilate, who sentenced him to be crucified.

14:55
Dan 6:4
1 Pet 3:16

14:56
Ps 35:11
Prov 6:16–19
19:5

14:58
Mk 15:29, 30
Jn 2:19

55 Inside, the chief priests and the whole Jewish Supreme Court were trying to find something against Jesus that would be sufficient to condemn him to death. But their efforts were in vain. 56 Many false witnesses volunteered, but they contradicted each other.

57 Finally some men stood up to lie about him and said, 58 "We heard him say, 'I will destroy this Temple made with human hands and in three days I will build another, made without human hands!' " 59 But even then they didn't get their stories straight!

60 Then the High Priest stood up before the Court and asked Jesus, "Do you refuse to answer this charge? What do you have to say for yourself?"

14:61
Isa 53:7
1 Pet 2:23

14:62
Ps 110:1
Dan 7:13
Mt 16:27; 24:30
Mk 8:38; 13:26
Acts 1:11
1 Thess 4:16
2 Thess 1:7
Rev 1:7; 22:20

14:63
Lev 24:15, 16
Jn 19:7
Acts 6:11

14:65
Isa 50:6; 53:5

61 To this Jesus made no reply.

Then the High Priest asked him. "Are you the Messiah, the Son of God?"

62 Jesus said, "I am, and you will see me sitting at the right hand of God, and returning to earth in the clouds of heaven."

63, 64 Then the High Priest tore at his clothes and said, "What more do we need? Why wait for witnesses? You have heard his blasphemy. What is your verdict?" And the vote for the death sentence was unanimous.

65 Then some of them began to spit at him, and they blindfolded him and began to hammer his face with their fists.

"Who hit you that time, you prophet?" they jeered. And even the bailiffs were using their fists on him as they led him away.

Peter denies knowing Jesus
(227/Matthew 26:69-75; Luke 22:54-65; John 18:25-27)

14:66
Mt 26:69–75
Lk 22:55–62
Jn 18:15–18 25–27

66, 67 Meanwhile Peter was below in the courtyard. One of the maids who worked for the High Priest noticed Peter warming himself at the fire.

She looked at him closely and then announced, "*You* were with Jesus, the Nazarene."

68 Peter denied it. "I don't know what you're talking about!" he said, and walked over to the edge of the courtyard.

Just then, a rooster crowed.

69 The maid saw him standing there and began telling the others, "There he is! There's that disciple of Jesus!"

14:70
Acts 2:7

70 Peter denied it again.

A little later others standing around the fire began saying to Peter, "You are, too, one of them, for you are from Galilee!"

14:62 *me*, literally, "the Son of Man." **14:68** *a rooster crowed*. This statement is found in only some of the manuscripts.

14:55 The Romans controlled Israel, but the Jews were given some power to handle religious and minor civil disputes. This Jewish ruling body, called the Supreme Court (or Sanhedrin), was made up of 71 of Israel's religious leaders. It was assumed that these men, as religious leaders, would be fair and just. Instead they showed great injustice in the trial of Jesus, even to the point of making up lies to use against him (verse 57).

14:58 This claim about which the false witnesses finally agreed twisted Jesus' actual words. He did not say, "I will destroy this Temple;" he said, "Destroy this sanctuary and in three days I will raise it up!" (John 2:19). Jesus was not talking about Herod's Temple, but about his own death and resurrection.

14:61–64 To the first question, Jesus made no reply because the evidence itself was confusing and erroneous. Not answering was wiser than trying to clarify the fabricated accusations. But if Jesus had refused to

answer the second question, it could have been taken as a denial of his mission. Instead, his answer predicted a powerful role-reversal. Sitting at the right hand of God meant he would come to judge *them* and they would be answering *his* questions (Psalm 110:1; Revelation 20:11–13).

14:63, 64 Of all people, the High Priest and other religious leaders should have recognized the Messiah because they knew the Scriptures thoroughly. Their job was to point people to God, but they were more concerned about their own reputations and holding onto what authority they had. They valued their human security more than their eternal security.

14:66, 67 Caiaphas' house, where Jesus was tried (verse 53), was part of a huge palace with several courtyards. John was apparently acquainted with the High Priest and some of his servants, and he was let into the courtyard along with Peter (John 18:15, 16).

71 He began to curse and swear. "I don't even know this fellow you are talking about," he said.

72 And immediately the rooster crowed the second time. Suddenly Jesus' words flashed through Peter's mind: "Before the cock crows twice, you will deny me three times." And he began to cry.

The council of religious leaders condemns Jesus
(228/Matthew 27:1, 2; Luke 22:66–71)

15 Early in the morning the chief priests, elders and teachers of religion— the entire Supreme Court—met to discuss their next steps. Their decision was to send Jesus under armed guard to Pilate, the Roman governor.

Jesus stands trial before Pilate
(230/Matthew 27:11–14; Luke 23:1–5; John 18:28–38)

2 Pilate asked him, "Are you the King of the Jews?"

"Yes," Jesus replied, "it is as you say."

3, 4 Then the chief priests accused him of many crimes, and Pilate asked him, "Why don't you say something? What about all these charges against you?"

5 But Jesus said no more, much to Pilate's amazement.

Pilate hands Jesus over to be crucified
(232/Matthew 27:15–26; Luke 23:13–25; John 18:39—19:16)

6 Now, it was Pilate's custom to release one Jewish prisoner each year at Passover time—any prisoner the people requested. 7 One of the prisoners at that time was Barabbas, convicted along with others for murder during an insurrection.

8 Now a mob began to crowd in toward Pilate, asking him to release a prisoner as usual.

9 "How about giving you the 'King of Jews'?" Pilate asked. "Is he the one

15:1 *the Roman governor,* implied.

14:71
Prov 29:25
1 Cor 10:12
14:72
2 Cor 7:10

15:1
Ps 2:2
Mt 27:1–26
Lk 22:66–23:3,
15–25
Jn 18:28–40
Acts 4:27

15:2
1 Tim 6:13

15:5
Isa 53:7
Jn 19:9
1 Pet 2:23

15:9
Ps 2:6
Jer 23:5, 6
Mic 5:2
Lk 1:31–33
Acts 3:13, 14

14:71 Peter's curse was more than just a common swear word. He was making the strongest denial he could think of by denying with an oath that he did not know Jesus. He said, in effect, "May God strike me dead if I'm lying."

14:71 It is easy to get angry at the Jewish Supreme Court for their injustice in condemning Jesus, but Peter and the rest of the disciples contributed to Jesus' pain by deserting him (verse 50). While most of us are not like the Jewish leaders, we are all like the disciples, for all of us have been guilty of denying Christ as Lord in vital areas of our life. We may pride ourselves that we have not committed certain sins, but we are all guilty of sin. Don't excuse yourself by pointing the finger at others whose sins seem worse than yours.

15:1 Why did the Jews send Jesus to Pilate, the Roman governor? The Romans had taken away the Jews' right to inflict capital punishment, so in order for Jesus to be condemned to death, he had to be sentenced by a Roman leader. More important, the Jewish leaders wanted Jesus executed on a cross, a method of death they believed brought a curse from God (see Deuteronomy 21:23). They hoped to persuade the people that Jesus was cursed, not blessed by God.

15:3, 4 The Jews had to fabricate new accusations against Jesus when they brought him before Pilate. The charge of blasphemy would mean nothing to the Roman governor, so they accused him of three other crimes: (1) encouraging the people not to pay their taxes to Rome, (2) claiming he was a king—"the King of the

Jews," and (3) causing riots all over the countryside. Tax evasion, treason, and terrorism—all of these would be cause for Pilate's concern.

15:5 Why didn't Jesus answer Pilate's questions? It would have been futile to answer, and the time had come to give his life to save the world. He had no reason to try to prolong the trial or save himself. His was the ultimate example of self-assurance and peace, which no ordinary criminal could imitate. Nothing would stop him from completing the work he had come to earth to do (Isaiah 53:7).

15:7 Barabbas was arrested for his part in a rebellion against the Roman government, and although he'd committed a murder, he may have been a hero among the Jews. The fiercely independent Jews hated to be ruled by pagan Romans. They hated paying taxes to support the despised government and its gods. Most of the Roman authorities, who had to settle Jewish disputes, hated the Jews in return. This period in history, therefore, was ripe for rebellion.

15:8 This mob was most likely a group of Jews loyal to the Jewish leaders. But where were the disciples and the crowds who days earlier had shouted, "Hail to the king" (11:9)? Jesus' sympathizers were afraid of the Jewish leaders, so they went into hiding. Another possibility is that the mob included many people who were in the Palm Sunday parade, but who turned against Jesus when they saw he was not going to be an earthly conqueror.

you want released?" ¹⁰(For he realized by now that this was a frameup, backed by the chief priests because they envied Jesus' popularity.)

¹¹But at this point the chief priests whipped up the mob to demand the release of Barabbas instead of Jesus.

¹²"But if I release Barabbas," Pilate asked them, "what shall I do with this man you call your king?"

¹³They shouted back, "Crucify him!"

In Jesus' day, any death sentence had to be approved by the top Roman official of the area. Pontius Pilate was in charge of the area where Jerusalem was located. When the Jewish leaders had Jesus in their power and wanted to kill him, their final obstacle was obtaining Pilate's permission. So it was that early one morning Pilate found a crowd at his door demanding a man's death.

Pilate's relationship with the Jews had always been stormy. His Roman toughness and fairness had been weakened by cynicism, compromises, and mistakes. On several occasions his actions had deeply offended the religious leaders. The resulting riots and chaos must have made Pilate wonder what he had gotten himself into. He was trying to control people who treated their Roman conquerors without respect. Jesus' trial was another episode in Pilate's ongoing problems.

For Pilate, there was never a doubt about Jesus' innocence. Three separate times he declared Jesus not guilty. He couldn't understand what made these people want to kill Jesus, but his fear of the pressure the Jews would place on him controlled his decision to allow Jesus' crucifixion. Because of their threat to inform the emperor that Pilate hadn't eliminated a rebel against Rome, Pilate went against what he knew was right. In desperation, he chose the opposite.

We share a common humanity with Pilate. At times we know the right and choose the wrong. He had his moment in history and now we have ours. What have we done with our opportunities and responsibilities? What judgment have we passed on Jesus?

Strengths and accomplishments:
• Roman governor of Judea

Weaknesses and mistakes:
• He failed in his attempt to rule a people who were defeated militarily but never dominated by Rome
• His constant political struggles made him a cynical and uncaring compromiser, susceptible to pressure
• Although he realized Jesus was innocent, he bowed to the public demand for his execution

Lessons from his life:
• Great evil can happen when truth is at the mercy of political pressures
• Resisting the truth leaves a person without purpose or direction

Key verse:
"What is truth?" Pilate exclaimed. Then he went out again to the people and told them, "He is not guilty of any crime. But you have a custom of asking me to release someone from prison each year at Passover. So if you want me to, I'll release the 'King of the Jews' " (John 18:38, 39).

Vital statistics:
Where: Judea
Occupation: Roman governor (or procurator) of Judea
Relatives: Wife, unnamed
Contemporaries: Jesus, Caiaphas, Herod

Pilate's story is told in the Gospels. He is also mentioned in Acts 3:13; 4:27; 13:28; 1 Timothy 6:13.

15:10 The Jews hated Pilate, but they went to him for the favor of condemning Jesus to crucifixion. Pilate could obviously see this was a frame-up. Why else would these people, who hated him and the Roman empire he represented, ask him to convict of treason and give the death penalty to one of their fellow Jews?

15:13 Crucifixion was the Roman penalty for rebellion. Only slaves or those who were not Roman citizens could be crucified. If Jesus died by crucifixion, he would die the death of a rebel and slave, not of the king he claimed to be. This is just what the Jewish religious leaders wanted as they whipped the mob into a frenzy. In addition, crucifixion would make it look as if the Romans were responsible for killing Jesus, and thus the religious leaders could not be blamed by the crowds.

¹⁴ "But why?" Pilate demanded. "What has he done wrong?" They only roared the louder, "Crucify him!"

¹⁵ Then Pilate, afraid of a riot and anxious to please the people, released Barabbas to them. And he ordered Jesus flogged with a leaded whip, and handed him over to be crucified.

15:15
Prov 29:25

Roman soldiers mock Jesus
(233/Matthew 27:27–31)

¹⁶, ¹⁷ Then the Roman soldiers took him into the barracks of the palace, called out the entire palace guard, dressed him in a purple robe, and made a crown of long, sharp thorns and put it on his head. ¹⁸ Then they saluted, yelling, "Yea! King of the Jews!" ¹⁹ And they beat him on the head with a cane, and spat on him and went down on their knees to "worship" him.

²⁰ When they finally tired of their sport, they took off the purple robe and put his own clothes on him again, and led him away to be crucified.

15:16
Mt 27:27–31
Jn 19:1–3, 16

Jesus is led away to be crucified
(234/Matthew 27:32–34; Luke 23:26–31; John 19:17)

²¹ Simon of Cyrene, who was coming in from the country just then, was pressed into service to carry Jesus' cross. (Simon is the father of Alexander and Rufus.)

²² And they brought Jesus to a place called Golgotha. (Golgotha means skull.) ²³ Wine drugged with bitter herbs was offered to him there, but he refused it. ²⁴ And then they crucified him—and threw dice for his clothes.

15:21
Mt 27:32–44
Lk 23:26–43
Jn 19:17–24
Rom 16:13
15:23
Ps 69:21
15:24
Ps 22:18

15:15 The region of Judea where Pilate ruled as governor was little more than a dusty outpost of the Roman empire. Because it was so far from Rome, Pilate was given just a small army. His primary job was to keep peace. We know from historical records that Pilate had already been warned about other uprisings in his region. Although he may have seen no guilt in Jesus and no reason to condemn him to death, he wavered when the Jews in the crowd threatened to report him to Caesar (John 19:12). Such a report, accompanied by a riot, could cost him his position and hopes for advancement.

15:15 Although Jesus was innocent according to Roman law, Pilate caved in under political pressure. He abandoned what he knew was right. He tried to second-guess the Jewish leaders and give a decision that would please everyone while keeping himself safe. When we lay aside God's clear statements of right and wrong and make decisions based on our audience, we fall into compromise and lawlessness. God promises to honor those who do right, not those who make everyone happy.

15:15 Who was guilty of Jesus' death? In reality, everyone was at fault. The disciples deserted him in fear. Peter denied that he even knew Jesus. Judas betrayed him. The crowds who had followed him stood by and did nothing. Pilate tried to blame the crowds. The religious leaders actively promoted Jesus' death. The Roman soldiers tortured him. If you had been there, watching these trials, what would your response have been?

15:21 Colonies of Jews existed outside Judea; Simon came from Cyrene in Africa, making a pilgrimage to Jerusalem for the Passover. His sons, Alexander and Rufus, are mentioned here because they evidently became well-known in the early church (Romans 16:13).

15:24 The dice the soldiers threw were used to decide,

by chance, who would receive Jesus' clothing. The Roman soldiers had the right to take for themselves the clothing of those crucified. This act fulfilled the prophecy of Psalm 22:18.

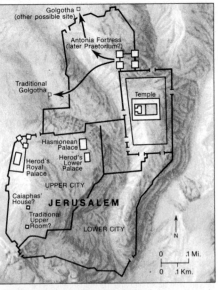

JESUS' ROUTE TO GOLGOTHA After being sentenced by Pilate, Jesus was taken from the Praetorium to a place outside the city, Golgotha, for crucifixion.

Jesus is placed on the cross
(235/Matthew 27:35–44; Luke 23:32–43; John 19:18–27)

15:25
Jn 19:14
15:26
Ps 2:6
Jer 23:5
Lk 1:31–33
15:28
Lk 22:37

15:29, 30
Ps 22:7
Mk 14:58
Jn 2:19
Acts 6:14

15:32
Heb 12:2, 3

²⁵ It was about nine o'clock in the morning when the crucifixion took place.

²⁶ A signboard was fastened to the cross above his head, announcing his crime. It read, "The King of the Jews."

²⁷ Two robbers were also crucified that morning, their crosses on either side of his. ²⁸ And so the Scripture was fulfilled that said, "He was counted among evil men."

²⁹, ³⁰ The people jeered at him as they walked by, and wagged their heads in mockery.

"Ha! Look at you now!" they yelled at him. "Sure, you can destroy the Temple and rebuild it in three days! If you're so wonderful, save yourself and come down from the cross."

³¹ The chief priests and religious leaders were also standing around joking about Jesus.

"He's quite clever at 'saving' others," they said, "but he can't save himself!"

³² "Hey there, Messiah!" they yelled at him. "You 'King of Israel'! Come on down from the cross and we'll believe you!"

And even the two robbers dying with him, cursed him.

Jesus dies on the cross
(236/Matthew 27:45–56; Luke 23:44–49; John 19:28–37)

15:33
Mt 27:45–56
Lk 23:44–49
Jn 19:28–30

³³ About noon, darkness fell across the entire land, lasting until three o'clock that afternoon.

15:28 This verse is omitted in some of the ancient manuscripts. The quotation is from Isa 53:12. **15:33** *the entire land,* or, "over the entire world."

WHY DID JESUS HAVE TO DIE?

The Problem	We have all done things that are wrong, and we have failed to obey God's law. Because of this, we have been separated from God our Creator. Separation from God is death; but, by ourselves, we can do nothing to become united with God.
Why Jesus Could Help	Jesus was not only a man; he was God's unique Son. Because Jesus never disobeyed God and never sinned, only he can bridge the gap between the sinless God and sinful mankind.
The Solution	Jesus freely offered his life for us, dying on the cross in our place, taking all our wrongdoing upon himself, and saving us from the consequences of sin—including God's judgment and death.
The Results	Jesus took our past, present, and future sins upon himself so that we could have new life. Because all our wrongdoing is forgiven, we are reconciled to God. Furthermore, Jesus' resurrection from the dead is the proof that his substitutionary sacrifice on the cross was acceptable to God, and his resurrection has become the source of new life for whoever believes that Jesus is the Son of God. All who believe in him may have this new life and live it in union with him.

15:25 Crucifixion was a feared and shameful form of capital punishment. The victim was forced to carry his cross along the longest possible route to the crucifixion site as a warning to the people. There were several shapes for crosses, as well as different methods of crucifixion. Jesus was nailed to the cross; condemned men were sometimes tied to their crosses with ropes. In either case, death came by suffocation because the weight of the body made breathing more and more difficult as the person lost strength.

15:26 A sign stating the condemned man's crime was often placed on a cross as a warning to the people. Because Jesus was never found guilty, the only accusation placed on his sign was the "crime" of being King of the Jews.

15:31 Jesus could have saved himself, but he endured this suffering because of his love for us. He could have chosen not to take the pain and humiliation; he could have killed those who mocked him—but he suffered through it all because he loved even his enemies. We had a significant part in the drama that afternoon because our sin was on the cross, too. Jesus died on that cross for us, and the penalty for our sin was paid by his death. The only adequate response we can make is to confess our sin and freely accept the fact that Jesus paid for it so we wouldn't have to. Don't insult God with indifference toward the greatest act of genuine love in history.

15:32 Luke records that one of these robbers repented before his death and Jesus promised him that he would be with him in Paradise (Luke 23:39–43).

34 Then Jesus called out with a loud voice, "Eli, Eli, lama sabachthani?" **15:34**
("My God, my God, why have you deserted me?")   Ps 22:1

35 Some of the people standing there thought he was calling for the prophet
Elijah. 36 So one man ran and got a sponge and filled it with sour wine and held **15:36**
it up to him on a stick.   Ps 69:21

"Let's see if Elijah will come and take him down!" he said.

37 Then Jesus uttered another loud cry, and dismissed his spirit.

38 And the curtain in the Temple was split apart from top to bottom.   **15:38**
                                                                      Ex 26:31–33
39 When the Roman officer standing beside his cross saw how he dismissed Eph 2:14
his spirit, he exclaimed, "Truly, this was the Son of God!"   Heb 6:19
                                                                      10:19, 20
40 Some women were there watching from a distance—Mary Magdalene,   **15:40**
Mary (the mother of James the Younger and of Joses), Salome, and others. Ps 38:11
                                                                      Lk 8:2
41 They and many other Galilean women who were his followers had
ministered to him when he was up in Galilee, and had come with him to
Jerusalem.

Jesus is laid in the tomb
(237/Matthew 27:57–61; Luke 23:50–56; John 19:38–42)

42, 43 This all happened the day before the Sabbath. Late that afternoon **15:42, 43**
Joseph from Arimathea, an honored member of the Jewish Supreme Court   Deut 21:22, 23
(who personally was eagerly expecting the arrival of God's Kingdom),   Mt 27:57–61
                                                                      Lk 2:25
gathered his courage and went to Pilate and asked for Jesus' body.   23:50–56
                                                                      Jn 19:38–42
44 Pilate couldn't believe that Jesus was already dead so he called for the
Roman officer in charge and asked him. 45 The officer confirmed the fact, and
Pilate told Joseph he could have the body.

46 Joseph bought a long sheet of linen cloth and, taking Jesus' body down **15:46**
from the cross, wound it in the cloth and laid it in a rock-hewn tomb, and Isa 53:9
                                                                      Acts 13:29
rolled a stone in front of the entrance.

15:34 *Eli, Eli, lama sabachthani.* He spoke here in Aramaic. The onlookers, who spoke Greek and Latin,
misunderstood his first two words ("Eloi, Eloi") and thought he was calling for the prophet Elijah.

15:34 Jesus did not ask this question in surprise or despair. He was quoting the first line of Psalm 22. The whole Psalm is a prophecy expressing the deep agony of the Messiah's death for the world's sin. Jesus knew this temporary separation from God would come the moment he took upon himself the sins of the world. This separation was what Jesus dreaded as he prayed in Gethsemane. The physical agony was horrible, but the spiritual separation from God was the ultimate pain.

15:37 This loud cry of Jesus was probably his last words, "It is finished" (John 19:30).

15:38 A heavy veil hung in front of the Temple room called the Holy of Holies, a place reserved by God for himself. Symbolically, the veil separated the holy God from sinful mankind. The room was entered only once a year, on the Day of Atonement, by the High Priest as he made a sacrifice to gain forgiveness for the sins of all the people. When Jesus died, the veil was split in two, showing that his death for our sins had opened up the way for us to approach our Holy God. Read Hebrews 9 for a more complete explanation of this.

15:42, 43 The Sabbath began at sundown on Friday and ended at sundown on Saturday. Jesus died just a few hours before sundown on Friday. It was against Jewish law to do physical work or to travel on the Sabbath. It was also against Jewish law to let a dead body remain exposed overnight (Deuteronomy 21:23). Joseph came to bury Jesus' body before the Sabbath began. If Jesus had died on the Sabbath when Joseph was unavailable, his body would have been taken down by the Romans. Had the Romans taken Jesus' body, no Jews could have

confirmed his death, and they could have disputed his resurrection.

15:42, 43 After Jesus died on the cross, Joseph of Arimathea asked for his body and then sealed it in a new tomb. Although an honored member of the Jewish Supreme Court, Joseph was a secret disciple of Jesus. Not all the religious leaders hated Jesus. Joseph risked his reputation as a religious leader to give a proper burial to the One he followed. It is frightening to risk one's reputation even for what is right. If your Christian witness endangers your reputation, consider Joseph. Today he is well known in the Christian church. How many of the other members of the Jewish Supreme Court can you name?

15:44 Pilate was surprised that Jesus had died so quickly, so he asked a soldier to double-check to make absolutely certain the report was true. Today, in an effort to deny the resurrection, there are those who say that Jesus didn't really die. His death, however, was confirmed by the soldier, Pilate, Joseph, the religious leaders, and the women who witnessed his burial. Jesus suffered true physical death on the cross.

15:46 This tomb was probably a man-made cave hewn from a hill and large enough to walk into. Joseph wrapped Jesus' body, placed it in the tomb, and rolled a heavy stone across the entrance. The religious leaders also watched where Jesus was buried, stationed guards by the tomb, and sealed the stone to make sure no one would try to steal Jesus' body and claim he had risen from the dead (Matthew 27:62–66).

[47] (Mary Magdalene and Mary the mother of Joses were watching as Jesus was laid away.)

Jesus rises from the dead
(239/Matthew 28:1–7; Luke 24:1–12; John 20:1–9)

16:1
Mt 28:1–8
Lk 24:1–10
Jn 20:1, 11–13

16 The next evening, when the Sabbath ended, Mary Magdalene and Salome and Mary the mother of James went out and purchased embalming spices.

Early the following morning, just at sunrise, they carried them out to the tomb. [3] On the way they were discussing how they could ever roll aside the huge stone from the entrance.

16:3
Mt 27:60
Mk 15:46

[4] But when they arrived they looked up and saw that the stone—a *very*

EVIDENCE THAT JESUS ACTUALLY DIED AND AROSE	Proposed Explanations for Empty Tomb	Evidence Against These Explanations	References
This evidence demonstrates Jesus' uniqueness in history and proves that he is God's Son. No one else was able to predict his own resurrection and then accomplish it.	Jesus was only unconscious and later revived.	A Roman soldier told Pilate Jesus was dead.	Mark 15:44, 45
		The Roman soldiers did not break Jesus' legs, because he had already died, and one of them pierced Jesus' side with a spear.	John 19:32–34
		Joseph of Arimathea and Nicodemus wrapped Jesus' body and placed it in the tomb.	John 19:38–40
	The women made a mistake and went to the wrong tomb.	Mary Magdalene and Mary the mother of Joses saw Jesus placed in the tomb.	Matthew 27:59–61 Mark 15:47 Luke 23:55
		On Sunday morning Peter and John also went to the same tomb.	John 20:3–9
	Unknown thieves stole Jesus' body.	The tomb was sealed and guarded by the Temple police and probably Roman soldiers, too.	Matthew 27:65, 66
	The disciples stole Jesus' body.	The disciples were ready to die for their faith. Stealing Jesus' body would have been admitting their faith was meaningless.	Acts 12:2
		The tomb was guarded and sealed.	Matthew 27:66
	The religious leaders stole Jesus' body to secure it.	If the religious leaders had taken Jesus' body, they would have produced it to stop the rumors of his resurrection.	none

15:47 These women could do very little—they couldn't speak before the Sanhedrin in Jesus' defense, they couldn't appeal to Pilate, they couldn't stand against the crowds, they couldn't overpower the Roman guards. But they did what they could. They stayed at the cross when the disciples had fled; they followed Jesus' body to its tomb; and they prepared spices for his body. Because they used the opportunities they had, they were the first to witness the resurrection. God blessed their devotion and diligence. As believers, we should take advantage of the opportunities we have and do what we *can* for Christ, instead of worrying about what we *cannot* do.

16:1, 2 The women purchased the spices on Saturday evening after the Sabbath had ended so they could go to the tomb early the next morning. The women did not want to use the spices for embalming Jesus' body, but for anointing it as a sign of love, devotion, and respect. Bringing spices to the tomb was like bringing flowers to a grave today.

16:4 The angels did not roll away the stone so Jesus could get out, but so others could get in and see for themselves that Jesus had indeed risen from the dead, just as he said.

heavy one—was already moved away and the entrance was open! ⁵So they entered the tomb—and there on the right sat a young man clothed in white. The women were startled, ⁶but the angel said, "Don't be so surprised. Aren't you looking for Jesus, the Nazarene who was crucified? He isn't here! He has come back to life! Look, that's where his body was lying. ⁷Now go and give this message to his disciples including Peter:

" 'Jesus is going ahead of you to Galilee. You will see him there, just as he told you before he died!' "

⁸The women fled from the tomb, trembling and bewildered, too frightened to talk.

16:5
John 20:11, 12
Acts 1:10; 10:30
16:6
Acts 2:23-32
Rom 1:3, 4
1 Cor 15:4, 12-20
2 Cor 5:15
1 Pet 1:3
Rev 1:18
16:7
Mt 26:32
Mk 14:28
Jn 21:1

Jesus appears to Mary Magdalene
(240/John 20:10-18)

⁹It was early on Sunday morning when Jesus came back to life, and the first person who saw him was Mary Magdalene—the woman from whom he had cast out seven demons. ¹⁰, ¹¹She found the disciples wet-eyed with grief and exclaimed that she had seen Jesus, and he was alive! But they didn't believe her!

16:9
Mt 28:9, 10
Lk 24:11
Jn 20:11-18

Jesus appears to two believers traveling on the road
(243/Luke 24:13-35)

¹²Later that day he appeared to two who were walking from Jerusalem into the country, but they didn't recognize him at first because he had changed his appearance. ¹³When they finally realized who he was, they rushed back to Jerusalem to tell the others, but no one believed them.

16:12
Lk 24:13-33
1 Cor 15:35-45
16:13
Lk 24:33-35

Jesus appears to the disciples including Thomas
(245/John 20:24-31)

¹⁴Still later he appeared to the eleven disciples as they were eating together. He rebuked them for their unbelief—their stubborn refusal to believe those who had seen him alive from the dead.

16:14
Lk 24:36
Jn 20:19-23
1 Cor 15:5

16:9 Vss 9-20 are not found in the most ancient manuscripts, but may be considered an appendix giving additional facts. **16:12** *Later that day*, literally, "after these things."

16:5 Mark says that one angel met the women at the tomb, while Luke records that there were two angels. These accounts are not contradictory. Each Gospel writer chose to highlight different details as he explained the same story, just as eyewitnesses to a news story each may highlight a different aspect of that event. Mark probably emphasized only the angel who spoke. The unique emphasis of each Gospel shows that they were written independently and that all four accounts are true and reliable.

16:6 The resurrection is vitally important for many reasons: (1) Jesus kept his promise to rise from the dead, so we can believe he will keep all his other promises. (2) The resurrection ensures that the ruler of God's eternal kingdom will be the living Christ, not just an idea, hope, or dream. (3) Christ rose from the dead, giving us the assurance that we also will be resurrected. (4) The power of God that brought Christ's body back from the dead is available to us to bring our morally and spiritually dead selves back to life so we can change and grow (1 Corinthians 15:12-19). (5) The resurrection provides the substance of the church's witness to the world. We do not merely tell lessons from the life of a good teacher; we proclaim the reality of the resurrection of Jesus Christ.

16:7 The angel made special mention of Peter to show that, in spite of Peter's denials, Jesus had not denied him. Jesus still had great responsibilities for Peter to fill in the church that was not yet born.

16:7 The angel told the disciples to meet Jesus in Galilee as Jesus had told them before (Mark 14:28). This is where he called most of them to be "fishers of men" (Matthew 4:19), and it would be where this mission would be restated (John 21). But the disciples, filled with fear, remained behind locked doors in Jerusalem (John 20:19). Jesus met them first in Jerusalem (Luke 24:36) and later in Galilee (John 21). Then he returned to Jerusalem where he ascended into heaven from the Mount of Olives (Acts 1:12).

16:13 When the two men finally realized who Jesus was, they rushed back to Jerusalem. It's not enough to read about Christ as a personality or to study his teachings. By believing that he is God, you trust him to save you and accept him as Lord of your life. This is the difference between knowing Jesus and knowing about him. Only when you know him will you be motivated to share with others what he has done for you.

Jesus gives the Great Commission
(248/Matthew 28:16–20)

16:15
Mt 28:16–20
Col 1:23

16:16
Jn 3:18, 36
12:48
Acts 2:38; 16:31
Rom 10:9
1 Pet 3:21

16:17
Lk 10:17
Acts 2:4; 19:6
1 Cor 12:10

16:18
Acts 5:16; 9:17
28:5

16:19
Lk 24:50, 51
Rom 8:34
Heb 1:3
Rev 3:21

¹⁵And then he told them, "You are to go into all the world and preach the Good News to everyone, everywhere. ¹⁶Those who believe and are baptized will be saved. But those who refuse to believe will be condemned.

¹⁷"And those who believe shall use my authority to cast out demons, and they shall speak new languages. ¹⁸They will be able even to handle snakes with safety, and if they drink anything poisonous, it won't hurt them; and they will be able to place their hands on the sick and heal them."

Jesus ascends into heaven
(250/Luke 24:50–53)

¹⁹When the Lord Jesus had finished talking with them, he was taken up into heaven and sat down at God's right hand.

²⁰And the disciples went everywhere preaching, and the Lord was with them and confirmed what they said by the miracles that followed their messages.

16:17 *speak new languages,* literally, "they will speak in new tongues." Some ancient manuscripts omit "new."

16:15 Jesus told his disciples to "go into all the world" telling everyone he paid the penalty for sin and that those who believe in him can be forgiven and live eternally with God. Christian disciples today are living in all parts of the world, telling this good news to people who haven't heard it. The driving power that carries missionaries around the world and sets Christ's church in motion is the faith that comes from the resurrection. Do you ever feel you don't have the skill or determination to be a witness for Christ? You must personally realize that Jesus rose from the dead and lives for you today. As you grow in your relationship with him, he will provide you with both the opportunities and the inner strength to tell his message.

16:16 It is not the water of baptism that saves, but God's grace accepted through faith in Christ. Baptism is an outward sign of inward faith. Because of Jesus' response to the thief on the cross who died with him, we know it is possible to be saved without being baptized (Luke 23:43). Baptism alone without faith does not automatically bring a person to heaven. Those who refuse to believe will be condemned, regardless of whether or not they have been baptized.

16:18 There are times when God intervenes miraculously to protect his followers. Occasionally he gives them special powers. Paul handled snakes safely (Acts 28:5), and the disciples healed the sick (Matthew 10:1; Acts 3:7, 8). This does not mean, however, that we should test God by putting ourselves in dangerous situations.

16:19 When Jesus ascended into heaven, his physical presence left the disciples (Acts 1:9). Jesus' sitting at God's right hand signifies the completion of his work, his authority as God, and his coronation as King.

16:20 Mark's Gospel emphasizes Christ's power as well as his servanthood. Jesus' life and teaching turn the world upside down. The world's view of power is to control others in order to get your way. But Jesus, with all authority and power in heaven and earth, chose to serve others. He held children in his arms, healed the sick, washed the disciples' feet, and died for the sins of the world. Following Jesus means receiving this same power to serve. We are called, as believers, to be servants of Christ. As Christ served, we are to serve.

250 EVENTS IN THE
LIFE OF CHRIST/
A HARMONY OF THE GOSPELS

All four books in the Bible that tell the story of Jesus Christ—Matthew, Mark, Luke, and John—stand alone, emphasizing a unique aspect of Jesus' life. But when these are blended into one complete account, or harmonized, we gain new insights about the life of Christ.

This harmony combines the four Gospels into a single chronological account of Christ's life on earth. It includes every chapter and verse of each Gospel, leaving nothing out.

The harmony is divided into 250 events. The title of each event is identical to the title found in the corresponding Gospel. Parallel passages found in more than one Gospel have identical titles, helping you to identify them quickly.

Each of the 250 events in the harmony is numbered. The number of the event corresponds to the number next to the title in the Bible text. When reading one of the Gospel accounts you will notice, at times, that some numbers are missing or out of sequence. The easiest way to locate these events is to refer to the harmony.

In addition, if you are looking for a particular event in the life of Christ, the harmony can help you locate it more rapidly than paging through all four Gospels. Each of the 250 events has a distinctive title keyed to the main emphasis of the passage to help you locate and remember the events.

This harmony will help you better visualize the travels of Jesus, study the four Gospels comparatively, appreciate the unity of their message, and strengthen your faith in Jesus.

I. BIRTH AND PREPARATION OF JESUS CHRIST

		Matthew	Mark	Luke	John
1	Luke's purpose in writing			1:1–4	
2	God became a human being				1:1–18
3	The ancestors of Jesus	1:1–17		3:23–38	
4	An angel promises the birth of John to Zacharias			1:5–25	
5	An angel promises the birth of Jesus to Mary			1:26–38	
6	Mary visits Elizabeth			1:39–56	
7	John the Baptist is born			1:57–80	
8	An angel appears to Joseph	1:18–25			
9	Jesus is born in Bethlehem			2:1–7	
10	Shepherds visit Jesus			2:8–20	
11	Mary and Joseph bring Jesus to the Temple			2:21–39	
12	Visitors arrive from eastern lands	2:1–12			
13	The escape to Egypt	2:13–18			
14	The return to Nazareth	2:19–23			
15	Jesus speaks with the religious teachers			2:41–52	
16	John the Baptist prepares the way for Jesus	3:1–12	1:1–8	3:1–18	
17	John baptizes Jesus	3:13–17	1:9–11	3:21, 22	
18	Satan tempts Jesus in the wilderness	4:1–11	1:12, 13	4:1–13	
19	John the Baptist declares his mission				1:19–28
20	John the Baptist proclaims Jesus as the Messiah				1:29–34
21	The first disciples follow Jesus				1:35–51
22	Jesus turns water into wine				2:1–12

II. MESSAGE AND MINISTRY OF JESUS CHRIST

	Matthew	Mark	Luke	John
23 Jesus clears the Temple				2:13–25
24 Nicodemus visits Jesus at night				3:1–21
25 John the Baptist tells more about Jesus				3:22–36
26 Herod puts John in prison			3:19, 20	
27 Jesus talks to a woman at the well				4:1–26
28 Jesus tells about the spiritual harvest				4:27–38
29 Many Samaritans believe in Jesus				4:39–42
30 Jesus preaches in Galilee	4:12–17	1:14, 15	4:14, 15	4:43–45
31 Jesus heals a government official's son				4:46–54
32 Jesus is rejected at Nazareth			4:16–30	
33 Four fishermen follow Jesus	4:18–22	1:16–20		
34 Jesus teaches with great authority		1:21–28	4:31–37	
35 Jesus heals Peter's mother-in-law and many others	8:14–17	1:29–34	4:38–41	
36 Jesus preaches throughout Galilee	4:23–25	1:35–39	4:42–44	
37 Jesus provides a miraculous catch of fish			5:1–11	
38 Jesus heals a man with leprosy	8:1–4	1:40–45	5:12–16	
39 Jesus heals a paralyzed man	9:1–8	2:1–12	5:17–26	
40 Jesus eats with sinners at Matthew's house	9:9–13	2:13–17	5:27–32	
41 Religious leaders ask Jesus about fasting	9:14–17	2:18–22	5:33–39	
42 Jesus heals a lame man by the pool				5:1–15
43 Jesus claims to be God's Son				5:16–30
44 Jesus supports his claim				5:31–47
45 The disciples pick wheat on the Sabbath	12:1–8	2:23–28	6:1–5	
46 Jesus heals a man's hand on the Sabbath	12:9–14	3:1–6	6:6–11	
47 Large crowds follow Jesus	12:15–21	3:7–12		
48 Jesus selects the twelve disciples		3:13–19	6:12–16	
49 Jesus gives the beatitudes	5:1–12		6:20–26	
50 Jesus teaches about salt and light	5:13–16			
51 Jesus teaches about the law	5:17–20			
52 Jesus teaches about anger	5:21–26			
53 Jesus teaches about lust	5:27–30			
54 Jesus teaches about divorce	5:31, 32			
55 Jesus teaches about vows	5:33–37			
56 Jesus teaches about retaliation	5:38–42			
57 Jesus teaches about loving enemies	5:43–48		6:27–36	
58 Jesus teaches about giving to the needy	6:1–4			
59 Jesus teaches about prayer	6:5–15			
60 Jesus teaches about fasting	6:16–18			
61 Jesus teaches about money	6:19–24			
62 Jesus teaches about worry	6:25–34			
63 Jesus teaches about criticizing others	7:1–6		6:37–42	
64 Jesus teaches about asking, seeking, knocking	7:7–12			
65 Jesus teaches about the way to heaven	7:13, 14			
66 Jesus teaches about fruit in people's lives	7:15–20		6:43–45	
67 Jesus teaches about those who build houses on rock and sand	7:24–29		6:46–49	
68 A Roman soldier demonstrates faith	8:5–13		7:1–10	
69 Jesus raises a widow's son from the dead			7:11–17	
70 Jesus eases John's doubt	11:1–19		7:18–35	
71 Jesus promises rest for the soul	11:28–30			
72 A sinful woman anoints Jesus' feet			7:36–50	
73 Women accompany Jesus and the disciples			8:1–3	
74 Religious leaders accuse Jesus of being Satan	12:22–37	3:20–30		
75 Religious leaders ask Jesus for a miracle	12:38–45			
76 Jesus describes his true family	12:46–50	3:31–35	8:19–21	
77 Jesus tells the parable of the four soils	13:1–9	4:1–9	8:4–8	
78 Jesus explains the parable of the four soils	13:10–23	4:10–25	8:9–18	
79 Jesus tells the parable of the growing seed		4:26–29		
80 Jesus tells the parable of the weeds	13:24–30			
81 Jesus tells the parable of the mustard seed	13:31, 32	4:30–34		
82 Jesus tells the parable of the yeast	13:33–35			
83 Jesus explains the parable of the weeds	13:36–43			
84 Jesus tells the parable of hidden treasure	13:44			

	Matthew	Mark	Luke	John
85 Jesus tells the parable of the pearl merchant	13:45, 46			
86 Jesus tells the parable of the fishing net	13:47–52			
87 Jesus calms the storm	8:23–27	4:35–41	8:22–25	
88 Jesus sends the demons into a herd of pigs	8:28–34	5:1–20	8:26–39	
89 Jesus heals a bleeding woman and restores a girl to life	9:18–26	5:21–43	8:40–56	
90 Jesus heals the blind and mute	9:27–34			
91 The people of Nazareth refuse to believe	13:53–58	6:1–6		
92 Jesus urges the disciples to pray for workers	9:35–38			
93 Jesus sends out the twelve disciples	10:1–15	6:7–13	9:1–6	
94 Jesus prepares the disciples for persecution	10:16–42			
95 Herod kills John the Baptist	14:1–12	6:14–29	9:7–9	
96 Jesus feeds five thousand	14:13–21	6:30–44	9:10–17	6:1–15
97 Jesus walks on water	14:22–33	6:45–52		6:16–21
98 Jesus heals all who touch him	14:34–36	6:53–56		
99 Jesus is the true bread from heaven				6:22–40
100 The Jews disagree that Jesus is from heaven				6:41–59
101 Many disciples desert Jesus				6:60–71
102 Jesus teaches about inner purity	15:1–20	7:1–23		
103 Jesus sends a demon out of a girl	15:21–28	7:24–30		
104 The crowd marvels at Jesus' healings	15:29–31	7:31–37		
105 Jesus feeds four thousand	15:32–39	8:1–9		
106 Religious leaders ask for a sign in the sky	16:1–4	8:10–12		
107 Jesus warns against wrong teaching	16:5–12	8:13–21		
108 Jesus restores sight to a blind man		8:22–26		
109 Peter says Jesus is the Messiah	16:13–20	8:27–30	9:18–20	
110 Jesus predicts his death the first time	16:21–28	8:31—9:1	9:21–27	
111 Jesus is transfigured on the mountain	17:1–13	9:2–13	9:28–36	
112 Jesus heals a demon-possessed boy	17:14–21	9:14–29	9:37–43	
113 Jesus predicts his death the second time	17:22, 23	9:30–32	9:44, 45	
114 Peter finds the coin in the fish's mouth	17:24–27			
115 The disciples argue about who would be the greatest	18:1–6	9:33–37	9:46–48	
116 The disciples forbid another to use Jesus' name		9:38–42	9:49, 50	
117 Jesus warns against temptation	18:7–9	9:43–50		
118 Jesus warns against looking down on others	18:10–14			
119 Jesus teaches how to treat a believer who sins	18:15–20			
120 Jesus tells the parable of the unforgiving debtor	18:21–35			
121 Jesus' brothers ridicule him				7:1–9
122 Jesus teaches about the cost of following him	8:18–22		9:57–62	
123 Jesus teaches openly at the Temple				7:10–31
124 Religious leaders attempt to arrest Jesus				7:32–53
125 Jesus forgives an adulterous woman				8:1–11
126 Jesus is the light of the world				8:12–20
127 Jesus warns of coming judgment				8:21–30
128 Jesus speaks about God's true children				8:31–47
129 Jesus states he is eternal				8:48-59
130 Jesus sends out seventy messengers			10:1–16	
131 The seventy messengers return			10:17–24	
132 Jesus tells the parable of the good Samaritan			10:25–37	
133 Jesus visits Mary and Martha			10:38–42	
134 Jesus teaches his disciples about prayer			11:1–13	
135 Jesus answers hostile accusations			11:14–28	
136 Jesus warns against unbelief			11:29–32	
137 Jesus teaches about the light within			11:33–36	
138 Jesus criticizes the religious leaders			11:37–54	
139 Jesus speaks against hypocrisy			12:1–12	
140 Jesus tells the parable of the rich fool			12:13–21	
141 Jesus warns about worry			12:22–34	
142 Jesus warns about preparing for his coming			12:35–48	

	Matthew	Mark	Luke	John
143 Jesus warns about coming division			12:49–53	
144 Jesus warns about the future crisis			12:54–59	
145 Jesus calls the people to repent			13:1–9	
146 Jesus heals the handicapped woman			13:10–17	
147 Jesus teaches about the Kingdom of God			13:18–21	
148 Jesus heals the man who was born blind				9:1–12
149 Religious leaders question the blind man				9:13–34
150 Jesus teaches about spiritual blindness				9:35–41
151 Jesus is the good shepherd				10:1–18
152 Religious leaders surround Jesus at the Temple				10:22–42
153 Jesus teaches about entering the Kingdom			13:22–30	
154 Jesus grieves over Jerusalem			13:31–35	
155 Jesus heals a man with dropsy			14:1–6	
156 Jesus teaches about seeking honor			14:7–14	
157 Jesus tells the parable of the great feast			14:15–24	
158 Jesus teaches about the cost of being a disciple			14:25–35	
159 Jesus tells the parable of the lost sheep			15:1–7	
160 Jesus tells the parable of the lost coin			15:8–10	
161 Jesus tells the parable of the lost son			15:11–32	
162 Jesus tells the parable of the shrewd accountant			16:1–13	
163 Jesus tells about the rich man and the beggar			16:19–31	
164 Jesus tells about forgiveness and faith			17:1–10	
165 Lazarus becomes ill and dies				11:1–16
166 Jesus comforts Mary and Martha				11:17–36
167 Jesus raises Lazarus from the dead				11:37–44
168 Religious leaders plot to kill Jesus				11:45–57
169 Jesus heals ten lepers			17:11–19	
170 Jesus teaches about the coming of the Kingdom of God			17:20–37	
171 Jesus tells the parable of the persistent widow			18:1–8	
172 Jesus tells the parable of two men who prayed			18:9–14	
173 Jesus teaches about marriage and divorce	19:1–12	10:1–12		
174 Jesus blesses little children	19:13–15	10:13–16	18:15–17	
175 Jesus speaks to the rich young man	19:16–30	10:17–31	18:18–30	
176 Jesus tells the parable of the workers paid equally	20:1–16			
177 Jesus predicts his death the third time	20:17–19	10:32–34	18:31–34	
178 Jesus teaches about serving others	20:20–28	10:35–45		
179 Jesus heals a blind beggar	20:29–34	10:46–52	18:35–43	
180 Jesus brings salvation to Zacchaeus' home			19:1–10	
181 Jesus tells the parable of the king's ten servants			19:11–27	
182 A woman anoints Jesus with perfume	26:6–13	14:3–9		12:1–11
183 Jesus rides into Jerusalem on a donkey	21:1–11	11:1–11	19:28–44	12:12–19
184 Jesus clears the Temple again	21:12–17	11:12–19	19:45–48	
185 Jesus explains why he must die				12:20–36
186 Most of the people do not believe in Jesus				12:37–43
187 Jesus summarizes his message				12:44–50
188 Jesus says the disciples can pray for anything	21:18–22	11:20–25		
189 Religious leaders challenge Jesus' authority	21:23–27	11:26–33	20:1–8	
190 Jesus tells the parable of the two sons	21:28–32			
191 Jesus tells the parable of the wicked farmers	21:33–46	12:1–12	20:9–19	
192 Jesus tells the parable of the wedding feast	22:1–14			
193 Religious leaders question Jesus about paying taxes	22:15–22	12:13–17	20:20–26	
194 Religious leaders question Jesus about the resurrection	22:23–32	12:18–27	20:27–40	
195 Religious leaders question Jesus about the greatest commandment	22:33–40	12:28–34		
196 Religious leaders cannot answer Jesus' question	22:41–46	12:35–37	20:41–44	

	Matthew	Mark	Luke	John
197 Jesus warns against the religious leaders	23:1–12	12:38–40	20:45–47	
198 Jesus condemns the religious leaders	23:13–36			
199 Jesus grieves over Jerusalem again	23:37–39			
200 A poor widow gives all she has		12:41–44	21:1–4	
201 Jesus tells about the future	24:1–22	13:1–20	21:5–24	
202 Jesus tells about his return	24:23–35	13:21–31	21:25–33	
203 Jesus tells about remaining watchful	24:36–51	13:32–37	21:34–38	
204 Jesus tells the parable of the ten bridesmaids	25:1–13			
205 Jesus tells the parable of the loaned money	25:14–30			
206 Jesus tells about the final judgment	25:31–46			

III. DEATH AND RESURRECTION OF JESUS CHRIST

	Matthew	Mark	Luke	John
207 Religious leaders plot to kill Jesus	26:1–5	14:1, 2	22:1, 2	
208 Judas agrees to betray Jesus	26:14–16	14:10, 11	22:3–6	
209 Disciples prepare for the Passover	26:17–19	14:12–16	22:7–13	
210 Jesus washes the disciples' feet				13:1–20
211 Jesus and the disciples have the Last Supper	26:20–29	14:17–25	22:14–30	13:21–30
212 Jesus predicts Peter's denial			22:31–38	13:31–38
213 Jesus is the way to the Father				14:1–14
214 Jesus promises the Holy Spirit				14:15–31
215 Jesus teaches about the vine and the branches				15:1–16
216 Jesus warns about the world's hatred				15:17—16:4
217 Jesus teaches about the Holy Spirit				16:5–16
218 Jesus teaches about using his name in prayer				16:17–33
219 Jesus prays for himself				17:1–5
220 Jesus prays for his disciples				17:6–19
221 Jesus prays for future believers				17:20–26
222 Jesus again predicts Peter's denial	26:30–35	14:26–31		
223 Jesus agonizes in the garden	26:36–46	14:32–42	22:39–46	
224 Jesus is betrayed and arrested	26:47–56	14:43–52	22:47–53	18:1–11
225 Annas questions Jesus				18:12–24
226 Caiaphas questions Jesus	26:57–68	14:53–65		
227 Peter denies knowing Jesus	26:69–75	14:66–72	22:54–65	18:25–27
228 The council of religious leaders condemns Jesus	27:1, 2	15:1	22:66–71	
229 Judas kills himself	27:3–10			
230 Jesus stands trial before Pilate	27:11–14	15:2–5	23:1–5	18:28–38
231 Jesus stands trial before Herod			23:6–12	
				18:39—
232 Pilate hands Jesus over to be crucified	27:15–26	15:6–15	23:13–25	19:16
233 Roman soldiers mock Jesus	27:27–31	15:16–20		
234 Jesus is led away to be crucified	27:32–34	15:21–24	23:26–31	19:17
235 Jesus is placed on the cross	27:35–44	15:25–32	23:32–43	19:18–27
236 Jesus dies on the cross	27:45–56	15:33–41	23:44–49	19:28–37
237 Jesus is laid in the tomb	27:57–61	15:42–47	23:50–56	19:38–42
238 Guards are posted at the tomb	27:62–66			
239 Jesus rises from the dead	28:1–7	16:1–8	24:1–12	20:1–9
240 Jesus appears to Mary Magdalene		16:9–11		20:10–18
241 Jesus appears to the women	28:8–10			
242 Religious leaders bribe the guards	28:11–15			
243 Jesus appears to two believers traveling on the road		16:12, 13	24:13–35	
244 Jesus appears to the disciples behind locked doors			24:36–43	20:19–23
245 Jesus appears to the disciples including Thomas		16:14		20:24–31
246 Jesus appears to the disciples while fishing				21:1–14
247 Jesus talks with Peter				21:15–25
248 Jesus gives the Great Commission	28:16–20	16:15–18		
249 Jesus appears to the disciples in Jerusalem			24:44–49	
250 Jesus ascends into heaven		16:19, 20	24:50–53	

Faith
—disciples not always strong in   *1:16–20*
—new believers can share it   *2:14, 15*
—impact of it   *4:30–32*
—how it was put into action   *5:32–34*
—when you are belittled for   *5:39, 40*
—taking the final step   *6:52*
—anything is possible with   *9:23*
—an attitude of trusting and believing   *9:24*
—a constant process   *9:24*
—prayer helps it   *9:29*
—having child-like faith   *10:14*
—wealth not always a by-product of   *10:26*
—faith without substance   *11:11–24*
—faith must endure to the end   *13:13*
Faithfulness
—remember God's   *9:50*
False Teachers
—how to recognize their deceptions   *13:22, 23*
Fame
—see Popularity
Family
—Jesus' family missed point of his ministry   *3:21*
—description of Jesus'   *3:31–35*
—Jesus talks about spiritual families   *3:31–35; 3:33–35*
Farm/Farmers/Farming
—laws for harvesting   *2:23*
—in Bible times   *4:3*
Fasting
—why John's disciples did, and Jesus disciples didn't   *2:18ff*
—purpose of   *2:18ff*
Fear
—how to resist it   *4:38–40*
—should not keep us from God   *5:25–34*
—letting Jesus deal with your   *6:50*
—disciples afraid to ask Jesus about his death   *9:32*
Fig/Fig Tree
—explanation of Jesus' curse of   *11:11–24*
—description of   *11:13–25*
Fishing
—in Jesus' day   *1:16*
Follow/Following
—why do you follow Jesus?   *3:7, 8*
—characteristics needed to follow Jesus   *3:14*
—submission required to follow Jesus   *8:34*
—following Jesus moment by moment   *8:34*
—you can choose to follow   *8:35*
Forgiveness
—admitting the need for   *1:5*
—accepting   *1:5*
—also mentioned in   *2:9–11*
Forsake/Forsaking
—Jesus asked why God had forsaken him   *15:34*
Foundation
—Jesus teaching is the church's   *12:10*
Fruit
—bearing spiritual fruit   *11:13–25*
Fulfill/Fulfillment
—Jesus fulfilled Old Testament law   *9:3ff*
Future
—God will keep his promises   *1:2, 3*
—depends upon how we live now   *12:24*
—Jesus talks about the end times   *13:3ff; 13:5–7*
—how to prepare for Jesus' return   *13:33, 34; 13:35*

Galilee, Region of
—description of   *1:39*
—where Jesus tells disciples to meet him   *16:7*
Galilee, Sea of
—storms on   *4:37, 38*

Gennesaret
—description of   *6:53*
Gentiles
—impact of Jesus' ministry on   *8:1*
Giving
—the spirit of   *12:41–44*
Goals
—Jesus' contrasted with Satan's   *5:10*
God's Word
—see Bible
Good News
—what it is   *1:14, 15*
—responsibility to share it   *6:11*
Gospel
—see Good News
Grain
—Jesus and disciples pick   *2:23*
Greatness
—in Jesus' eyes   *9:36–42*
—true greatness   *10:42–44*
Growth
—understanding the process of spiritual growth   *4:26–29*
—gradual, not instant   *9:30, 31*
—spiritual barrenness   *11:13–25*

Handicaps
—in Jesus' day   *10:46*
Harvest
—laws for harvesting to help the poor   *2:24*
Healing
—on the Sabbath   *1:32, 33; 3:4*
—Jesus heals a blind man   *8:25*
Heart
—keeping it open and pliable for God   *2:21, 22; 8:17, 18*
—Jesus requires willing heart   *3:14*
—hard hearts of Pharisees   *8:11; 8:15ff*
Heaven
—values found there   *10:31*
—can't look at it from human perspective   *12:24*
—relationships in   *12:25*
—see also Kingdom of God
Helping
—helping others a priority   *9:38*
Herod Antipas
—Profile of   *chpt. 6*
Herodians
—chart describing   *chpt. 2*
—description of   *3:6*
—why Jesus was a threat to   *3:6; 12:13*
Herodias
—why she wanted John the Baptist killed   *6:17–19*
History
—why Jesus came when he did   *1:2*
—God reveals his plans for   *1:2, 3*
Holy/Holiness
—pretending to be holy   *7:6, 7*
Holy Spirit
—baptism of   *1:8*
—in the Trinity   *1:10, 11*
—blasphemy against   *3:28, 29*
Hope
—in the midst of crisis   *5:36*
Horrible Thing
—description of   *13:14*
Houses
—description of   *2:4*
Human/Humanness
—Jesus fully God and fully human   *1:12, 13*
Humility
—baptism demonstrates   *1:8*
—fasting a sign of   *2:18ff*

Peter
—called as a disciple *1:16–20*
—viewed Jesus wrongly *8:32, 33*
—why Jesus scolded him *8:33*
—among inner circle of disciples *9:2*
—also mentioned in *9:1; 9:9, 10*
Pharisee/Pharisees
—what made them reject Jesus' message *2:21, 22; 12:13*
—accuse Jesus of harvesting on the Sabbath *2:24*
—chart describing *chpt. 2*
—hypocrisy of *3:4*
—description of *3:6*
—Jesus a threat to *3:6*
—refusal to believe Jesus' miracles *3:22–26*
—why they were hypocrites *7:6, 7*
—added to God's laws *7:8, 9*
—why they demanded a miracle *8:11*
—how they tried to trap Jesus about divorce *10:2*
—how they tried to trap Jesus regarding authority *11:26–30*
—their true motives exposed *12:38–40*
—see also Religious Leaders
Phoniness
—how we become phonies *12:38–40*
Pigs
—considered unclean by Jews *5:11*
Pilate
—profile of *chpt. 15*
—why Jesus was sent to him *15:1*
—why Jesus didn't answer his questions *15:5*
—why religious leaders sent Jesus to *15:10*
—why he condemned Jesus *15:15*
—bows to political pressure *15:15*
Plans
—God reveals his plans through history *1:2, 3*
Planting
—used to illustrate growth of God's word *4:3*
Pleasure
—what Jesus said about it *8:36, 37*
Politics
—Jesus exposed political ambitions of religious leaders *3:6*
—truth should not be subject to *Pilate's profile, Key lessons chpt. 15*
—Pilate bows to political pressure *15:15*
Pontius Pilate
—see Pilate
Poor
—laws to farmers for helping *2:23*
Popularity
—religious leaders jealous of Jesus' *3:2*
—Jesus' increasing *3:7, 8*
Position
—see Reputation/Position
Possessions
—should you give yours away? *10:21*
Power
—valuing it higher than God *3:2*
—Pharisees said Jesus' came from Satan *3:22–26*
—of Jesus *5:41, 42; 7:29*
Prayer
—finding time to pray *1:35*
—can we pray for anything? *9:23; 10:38*
—keys to effective *9:29*
—conditions of *11:22, 23*
—Jesus' prayer in the Garden *14:35, 36*
Prejudice
—blinds us to the truth *6:2, 3*
Preparation
—John the Baptist prepared people for Jesus *1:5*

—preparing for Christ's return *13:33, 34; 13:35*
Pressure
—combating pressure to do wrong *6:20*
—makes us vulnerable to temptation *14:41*
Pride
—prevented Pharisees from believing in Jesus *3:22–26*
—barrier to belief in Jesus *6:5*
—how it affects our values *9:34*
—often a result of wealth *10:17–23*
Promises
—comfort in knowing God keeps them *1:2, 3*
Problems
—trusting God in *4:38–40*
—how we underestimate Jesus' help in *4:41*
—should not keep us from God *5:25–34*
—hope in the midst of *5:36*
—God hasn't lost sight of your *6:49*
Proof
—Jesus' actions proved who he is *1:1*
Prophecy
—Jesus puts it in perspective *13:3ff; 13:35*
—Jesus tells about the end times *13:3ff; 13:5–7*
Prophets
—Israel looking for *1:2*
—importance of their predictions about Jesus *1:2, 3*
—Jesus surpasses their authority and power *9:3ff*
—their prophecies of the Messiah misunderstood *10:37*
Punishment
—of religious leaders to be greater *12:40*
Purpose
—following rules but missing their purpose *2:24*
—religious leaders lost sight of their real purpose *3:2*

Ransom
—explanation of *10:45*
—Jesus paid for us *10:45*
Readiness
—some not yet ready to receive God's message *4:11, 12*
—asking God to make others ready to receive his message *4:11, 12*
Rebellion
—Israel ripe for *15:7*
Rejection
—consequences of rejecting Jesus *3:28, 29*
—people's rejection vs. Jesus' acceptance *6:4*
—teamwork helps us deal with *6:7*
Relationships
—among members of God's family *3:33–35*
—in heaven *12:25*
Religious leaders
—their authority contrasted to Jesus' *1:22*
—accuse Jesus of healing on the Sabbath *1:32, 33*
—shun lepers *1:40, 41*
—accuse Jesus of blasphemy *2:7*
—chart of prominent groups *chpt. 2*
—missed true purpose of the Sabbath *2:24; 2:27, 28*
—why they turned against Jesus *3:2; 12:13*
—guilty of blasphemy *3:28, 29*
—why Jesus sometimes avoided confronting *5:43*
—Jesus accuses *7:1ff*
—kept the law for the wrong reasons *7:1ff*
—added to God's laws *7:8, 9*
—Jesus exposed true motives of *12:1ff; 12:17; 12:38–40*
—try to trap Jesus with tax question *12:14*
—why their judgment will be greater *12:40*
—plot to kill Jesus *14:1*
—trial of Jesus *14:53ff; 14:55*
—explanation of their Supreme Court *14:55*
—fabricate charges against Jesus *15:3, 4*

—why they sent Jesus to Pilate *15:10*
—also mentioned in *5:19*
—see also Pharisees, Sadducees
Renewal
—the value of *6:31*
Repentance
—John's baptism a sign of *1:4; 1:5*
—fasting a sign of *2:18ff*
Reputation/Position
—should not get in the way of witnessing *2:16, 17*
—valuing it higher than God *3:2*
—what true greatness is *10:42–44*
—risking it for Jesus *15:42, 43*
Resist/Resistance
—different ways people resist God's Word *4:14–20*
Respond/Response
—different ways people respond to God *4:14–20*
Responsibility
—to use what we have *4:25*
—for how you respond to the gospel *6:11*
—for sharing the gospel *6:11*
Rest
—the value of *6:31*
Resurrection
—Jesus proves there will be *12:26*
—why it is important for our faith *16:6*
—the reason for sharing our faith *16:15*
Rewards
—don't come without suffering *8:32, 33*
—how to receive heavenly *10:29, 30*
Riches
—see Wealth; Money
Robbers
—on the crosses beside Jesus *15:33*
Rock
—Jesus calls himself *12:10*
Roman Empire
—how it helped spread the Gospel *1:2*
—pagan influence of *1:21*
Rome/Romans
—troops stationed in Nazareth *1:9*
—little respect for God *1:9*
—Capernaum a key headquarters *2:14*
—Jews looked for political savior from *3:12*
—how it divided Israel *6:17–19*
—Herodians fearful of *12:13*
—Why Jews hated paying taxes to *2:14; 12:14*
—constant tension with Jews *15:7*
—also mentioned in *9:12, 13; 10:37*
Rules
—missing their true intent *2:24*

Sabbath
—Jesus accused of breaking *1:32, 33; 2:24*
—religious leaders missed true purpose of *2:24; 2:27, 28*
—Jesus accused of healing on *3:4*
Sacrifice
—putting pleasure in perspective *8:36, 37*
—Jesus is worth any sacrifice *9:43ff*
—the final sacrifice *14:24*
Sadducees
—chart describing *chpt. 2*
—try to trap Jesus with legal question *12:18*
—beliefs about the resurrection *12:26*
Salt
—what it illustrates *9:50*
Salvation
—knowing about Jesus not enough for *3:11*
Sanhedrin
—see Supreme Court

Satan
—description of *1:12, 13*
—tempted Jesus *1:12, 13*
—rules demons *1:23*
—Pharisees said Jesus' power came from *3:22–26*
—God's control of *3:27*
—his goals contrasted with Jesus' *5:10*
—why Jesus called Peter this *8:33*
—our ongoing battle with *9:18*
—defeated by Christ's death *14:27*
School
—synagogue as *5:22*
Scribes
—chart describing *chpt. 2*
Seed
—parable of the mustard seed *4:30–32*
Servanthood
—Jesus' example of *16:20*
Separation
—how Jews showed separation from pagan influences *6:11*
Selfish/Selfishness
—pursuit of pleasure *8:36, 37*
Self-sufficiency
—impossible without Christ *9:24*
Self-centered
—why it is destructive *8:35*
Shepherd
—Jesus compared to *6:34*
Sickness/Disease
—of the woman who touched Jesus *5:25–34*
Sidon
—description of *7:24*
Simon of Cyrene
—why he was in Jerusalem *15:21*
Sin
—how it deforms our character *1:40, 41*
—a greater enemy than persecution *3:12*
—wrong words can lead to *6:22, 23*
—begins with attitudes and thoughts *7:18, 7:20–23*
—our own efforts not enough to defeat *9:18*
—responsibility to confront it *9:42*
—ruthlessly removing it *9:43ff*
—consequences of *9:48, 49*
Society
—how it is contaminated by sin *8:15ff*
Soil
—parable of the four soils explained *4:14–20*
Son of Man
—see Jesus
Sower/Sowing
—parable of sower explained *4:14–20*
—see also Farm/Farmer/Farming
Status
—see Reputation
Storm/Storms
—on Sea of Galilee *4:37, 38*
Stress
—makes us vulnerable to temptation *14:41*
Stubborn/Stubborness
—a detriment to Jesus' life-changing message *2:21, 22*
Submit/Submission
—Jesus illustrates *8:34, 8:35*
Success
—disciples preoccupied with *9:34*
Suffering
—rewards don't come without *8:32, 33*
—why Jesus had to suffer *9:12, 13*
—developing a willing attitude about *10:38*
—why Jesus suffered for us *15:31*